For our tag-team partners Jaxon and Noah

A BATTLE ROYAL IN THE SKY

THE LIFE AND DEATH OF WRESTLING'S 100 GREATEST GODS AND GIMMICKS

Pitch Publishing Ltd
A2 Yeoman Gate
Yeoman Way
Durrington
BN13 3QZ

Email: info@pitchpublishing.co.uk
Web: www.pitchpublishing.co.uk

First published by Pitch Publishing 2012
Text © 2012 Jon Chattman and Rich Tarantino
Photography: wrealano@aol.com

13-digit ISBN: 9781908051141
Design and typesetting by Brilliant Orange Sports Management.
Printed in Spain by GraphyCems. Manufacturing managed by Jellyfish Print Solutions Ltd.

A BATTLE ROYAL IN THE SKY

THE LIFE AND DEATH OF WRESTLING'S 100 GREATEST GODS AND GIMMICKS

JON CHATTMAN & RICH TARANTINO

FOREWORD BY AL SNOW

AFTERWORD BY TERRY FUNK

pitch

CONTENTS

FOREWORD RUN-IN

Jon and Rich Tarantino are good bruddas. Rich came up with the idea for this book, and he and Jon make a great tag team. They wrote that funny mustache book Sweet Stache. This wrestling book remembers many who have died, and many bad gimmicks. We have lost many greats. I am very sad when I hear that a young guy passed away because of drugs or whatever. I wish I could have helped them all, brudda. As far as gimmicks, this brudda never needed one. I saw some pretty bad gimmicks out there, but the Superfly wasn't one of them!

Jimmy "Superfly" Snuka

FOREWORD BY AL SNOW

I met Jon when he contacted me about doing an interview for a magazine. It was quickly apparent to me throughout the course of the interview that Jon and I had many similar interests and as such were destined to become friends.

For instance, both Jon and I have a strong sense of community service and patriotism. For example, we both do magic acts for the blind (quick note: they love card tricks: you just have to say 'Ta Dah' after every trick) and Jon and I are both tyrannical despots of Third World countries. (Quick note: 'Long Live Canada'... What, I told you I was patriotic.)

Jon and I also enjoy physical competition and will fight a small farm animal for money at the drop of a hat. (Quick note: Jon always says, 'Find me a farm and I will find

a fight.') As uncanny as the two of us sharing all of that was, Jon and I also connected in our deep reverence and respect for two of the most amazing television actors of all time… Patrick Duffy and Simon McCorkindale. Now I know what you're thinking – Patrick Duffy and Simon McCorkindale? – and Jon and I would say emphatically YES.

Not just any thespian can bring to life the classic television characters of *The Man from Atlantis* and *Manimal* respectively and continue to not only have a career, but yet reach even greater heights when one would believe they had already reached their zenith.

But what truly bonded Jon and I was our true love of the art form of professional wrestling, and yes, I did say 'art form'. Aside from jazz, the only truly American-created art form that the rest of the world has used as a template for their own endeavours. The art of physical storytelling; of competition of good versus evil; a true passion play that has been and always will be a reflection of the very society we live in.

During the course of the aforementioned interview I could see and hear the passion and respect that Jon held for what I had too often found as a maligned and scorned segment of the entertainment industry that I had pursued as a career.

Now don't get me wrong – the wrestling business has certainly earned its fair share of it on its own. With scandals ranging from steroids and illicit and illegal drug use to the tragic litany of premature deaths of its performers. If you've bought this book because of those things then you will be disappointed. This book does not focus on the negative or dark side of the professional wrestling business. This book does not ignore it but instead focuses on the personal triumphs and successes of those performers. On the gimmicks that worked and the ones that failed miserably. (Quick note: a personal favourite Avatar – 'Like the proverbial fart in church.')

At times this book will make you laugh, but will always be poignant and make you appreciate the performers and their colourful careers and exploits. At times, this book takes the reader and fan in all of us back to when we sat down on the living room floor on Saturday mornings with our bowl of cereal and got lost in the wonderful, wild, wacky and magical world of professional wrestling.

I believe that you the reader will not only realise Jon's and his co-author Rich Tarantino's (quick note: I do not know if Rich is any relation to Quentin as that fact was not brought up in his profile that aired on *America's Most Wanted*) mastery of the written word and possibly learn something you did not know along the way about professional wrestling, but you will also see and feel their love for the art form of professional wrestling. In doing so, you may begin to develop your own love for it too.

Enjoy!

DEDICATION

I became a pro wrestling fan thanks to Cyndi Lauper's 'The Goonies R Good Enough' music video, which featured various World Wrestling Federation superstars making hilarious cameo appearances. Drawn in by the quirkiness of it all, I quickly became a fan of the WWF (now WWE) men in tights. I couldn't wait to see what Bobby 'The Brain' Heenan or 'Rowdy' Roddy Piper would say or what opponent (and turnbuckle) George 'The Animal' Steele would devour next. Right from the get-go, however, two stars resonated most with me. Obviously, no child of the 1980s could live his life without idolising Hulk Hogan. I was no different – a true Hulkamaniac who even tried making a few protein shakes. But the Hulkster wasn't my only idol. Randy 'Macho Man' Savage sucked me in with his wrestling style, unpredictable behaviour, and even more impressive mic skills. (The lovely Miss Elizabeth didn't hurt either.) Before long, I had his T-shirt, a 7-Eleven 'Big Gulp' with his caricature on it, and even tried snapping into a Slim Jim, no matter how gross they tasted.

I remember in the late 1980s, my father would take me to WWF matches no matter how near or far away they were based and a constant main event was Savage versus long-time rival Ricky 'The Dragon' Steamboat. (My dad was a good sport – he wasn't a fan but knew how much I was of all things WWF.) Both Savage and Steamboat were notoriously known throughout the industry (watch WrestleMania III now) as the best in the business and they clearly didn't disappoint. I loved every minute of it, and appreciated the father/son male bonding over body slams and elbow drops.

By the early 1990s, I stopped watching wrestling because I felt it was time to grow up. By 1997, my senior year of college, however, I was sucked back in by... yes, Savage and Hogan. At the nudging of my best friend Steve I was talked into watching World Championship Wrestling (WCW) because all the

photo:Wrealano@aol.com

There will never be another Randy Savage. Without him, there would be no 'Stone Cold' Steve Austin or 'heels' you could root for. As a wrestler, I idolised him. As a man, I respected him. Long live the 'Macho King'.

1980s icons were back on TV – reinventing the genre and kicking WWF's ass. By 2001, WCW was over but Savage was not. He filmed a cameo as Bonesaw McGraw in Sam Raimi's *Spider-Man*, and I was fortunate to land an interview for a Marvel publication I freelanced for. I found out quite fittingly. While at Opening Day with my father watching the New York Mets, I decided to check my voicemail. 'Jon Chattman... this is Randy "Macho Man" Savage.'

The wrestling icon's attorney let him know I wanted to interview him, and called me to set it up. When I called him back later that day, all the memories from my dad and I going to matches came back to me. Once I interviewed him, I was beside myself. We hit it off instantly and for over an hour he talked the squared circle, Spidey, and his early days of minor league baseball. He also told me how he got the 'Macho Man' moniker. In the weeks leading up to the article's pub date, I spoke with Savage roughly once a week. Once it was printed, those phone calls continued. He'd

often call asking for copies of the magazine. (Meanwhile, while all this was happening, I changed my voicemail at work to Macho's voice saying, 'Jon Chattman'.)

Macho and I eventually met in Orlando on a weekend we were, coincidentally, both in town. On the phone, Savage was his in-ring persona. He talked to me just like he talked to 'Mean Gene' Okerlund, and when we met face to face, it was just the same. We met in a hotel lobby and I saw him coming to me from a mile away. He pointed from far away (as he had to so many opponents), gave me the firmest handshake of my life, and we ate lunch. He ordered a 'New York Reuben' in honour of 'my New York friend' (me), and we talked everything from his near-purchase of WCW to his on-and-off again friendship with the Hulkster. I also told him about the days of me going to the Meadowlands or New York-area arenas with my father, and watching him perform at arguably the peak of his career. Always humble and surprisingly down-to-earth, Savage smiled at me, raised his beer, and said, 'I'll drink to that.' After he picked up the lunch bill, we shook hands once more and he thanked me again for the article. He even met some of my friends and took photos with them. Weeks later, he sent signed photos calling me 'the man' and thanking me again.

We talked on the phone a few times after that, but ultimately lost touch. For years, I'd tried to contact him to no avail. Two years after interviewing Savage, I ended up interviewing Hogan. I remember how proud I was of myself that I got to interview the wrestling 'Mega Powers' – my two childhood role models not named 'dad'.

Savage's death hit me hard, and that's saying a lot considering how many wrestlers from that glorious era have died tragically. Not only was Savage a part of my childhood and personified the strong relationship I have with my father, but he lived up to the hype when I met him.

There will never be another Randy Savage. Without him, there would be no 'Stone Cold' Steve Austin or 'heels' you could root for. As a wrestler, I idolised him. As a man, I respected him. Long live the 'Macho King'.

* Originally written by Jon Chattman on May 5, 2011, for the *Huffington Post*

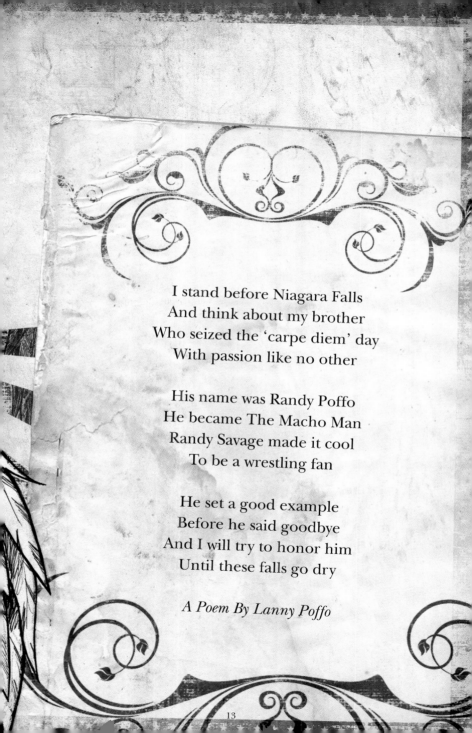

I stand before Niagara Falls
And think about my brother
Who seized the 'carpe diem' day
With passion like no other

His name was Randy Poffo
He became The Macho Man
Randy Savage made it cool
To be a wrestling fan

He set a good example
Before he said goodbye
And I will try to honor him
Until these falls go dry

A Poem By Lanny Poffo

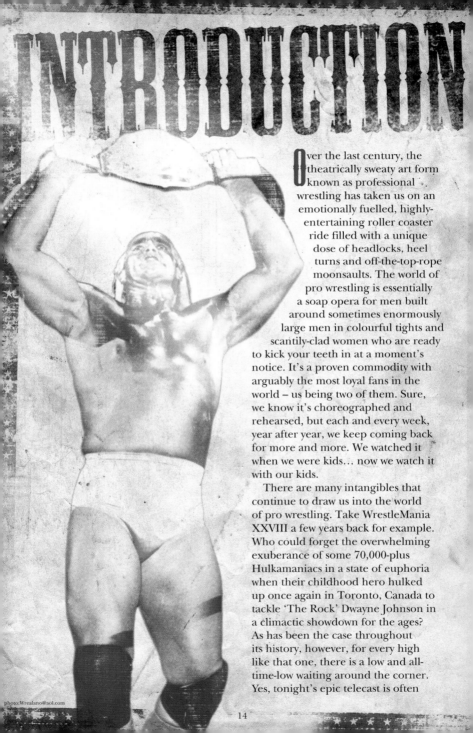

INTRODUCTION

Over the last century, the theatrically sweaty art form known as professional wrestling has taken us on an emotionally fuelled, highly-entertaining roller coaster ride filled with a unique dose of headlocks, heel turns and off-the-top-rope moonsaults. The world of pro wrestling is essentially a soap opera for men built around sometimes enormously large men in colourful tights and scantily-clad women who are ready to kick your teeth in at a moment's notice. It's a proven commodity with arguably the most loyal fans in the world – us being two of them. Sure, we know it's choreographed and rehearsed, but each and every week, year after year, we keep coming back for more and more. We watched it when we were kids… now we watch it with our kids.

There are many intangibles that continue to draw us into the world of pro wrestling. Take WrestleMania XXVIII a few years back for example. Who could forget the overwhelming exuberance of some 70,000-plus Hulkamaniacs in a state of euphoria when their childhood hero hulked up once again in Toronto, Canada to tackle 'The Rock' Dwayne Johnson in a climactic showdown for the ages? As has been the case throughout its history, however, for every high like that one, there is a low and all-time-low waiting around the corner. Yes, tonight's epic telecast is often overshadowed by tomorrow's weak storyline, gimmick gone wrong, or unfortunate tragedy out of the ring. Speaking of which, pro wrestling has had its fair share of tragic events over the years. Too often a wrestling legend, no matter the circumstance, is taken from us way too soon. We all know where we were when Owen Hart, dressed in his Blue Blazer guise, plunged to his death at a pay-per-view event, and similarly recall the tragic news surrounding Chris Benoit. Those are two examples of a bottomless outside-the-ring storyline surrounding wrestlers' deaths. Like many of those before and after, these superstars will never ever be forgotten. They are a part of the rich-storied history of wrestling.

On a much lighter note, the pro wrestling world has, over the decades, gone through its fair share of peaks, valleys, and Sean Mooneys. Around every corner, promoters and sports entertainment writers are trying to come up with that next big original hook or the next big gimmick in order to help reel in audiences. While some break out – take a Sheamus or Batista – many turn up limp. In other words, for every 'Stone Cold' Steve Austin created, 9 out of 10 times the powers that be shit the bed and pooped out a Doink the Clown.

As history has shown, the constant seesaw of wrestling will continue. New stars will emerge, past favourites will pass, and more gimmicks will grow. As we look ahead or dread, as fans, what the future may bring, this book wants to bring you back to those wrestlers and memories we've lost.

This book celebrates the lives of our heroes in tights who passed away before their prime. For an industry full of its fair share of tragedy, we focus on how 50 of our dearly departed lived their lives in the squared circle. We also take a look at 50 gimmicks and storylines that aren't around anymore – whether that's for the good, the bad, or the Man Mountain Rock ugly.

It's time now to enter a battle royal in the sky.

THE DAY COMPETITION DIED

Everyone remembers, 'the day the music died'. The Big Bopper, Richie Valens and Buddy Holly perished in a small plane crash, and Don McLean sang all about it in 'American Pie'. Another sad day in history – at least in professional wrestling history – was when Vince McMahon hammered the final nail in the WCW coffin.

On March 23, 2001, World Wrestling Federation Entertainment (now World Wrestling Entertainment) acquired their biggest competitor, World Championship Wrestling, including all global rights of the brand and their entire library of vintage classic matches. This day will live in infamy because it was the day pure wrestling competition died. Sure, mixed martial arts may slightly challenge the WWE's ratings now and TNA continues to sign veteran big names in an effort to steal some thunder, but legitimate competition is as dead as Al Snow's Avatar gimmick.

WCW and WWE feuded for some 20 years, vying for fans' attention, stealing each other's talent – especially at the height of the 'Monday Night Wars' of the 1990s, and going neck-and-neck in the ratings. Sure, WWE had the edge most of the time, but WCW brought its A-game with stars like Magnum TA and the legendary Ric Flair. But that latter statement refers to the 1980s.

photo:Wrealano@aol.com

Let's get back to the 1990s, when there was no better time to be a wrestling fan. The 1990s were unpredictable – which in wrestling is rare. Fans never knew which face would turn heel or which WWE star might turn up on WCW programming on any given night. I was like a kid in a candy shop every single Monday night switching back and forth from station to station to catch what was going to happen next, what moment to savour (remember The Rock N Sock Connection?) and what moments to spit out (sorry, Das Wunderkind.)

This golden era of wrestling, unfortunately, overstayed its welcome and by 2001, WCW was limping in the ratings and real stars. Vampiro just didn't cut it.

The final WCW Monday Nitro saw a storyline in which Shane McMahon purchased WCW from underneath his father's guise. It led to a limp storyline in which C-level WCW stars 'invaded' WWE. Stars like Lance Storm, Booker T and Buff Bagwell (for a night anyway) couldn't help the brand stay alive and after a string of attempts, McMahon ultimately decided to shut down the existence of the brand. Past WCW icons joined WWE over the years such as Ric Flair, Big Poppa Pump Scott Steiner, and Goldberg, but only the 'Nature Boy' had a strong run on WWE programming and it never really felt the same. In wrestling, competition is king. It raises every organisation to a higher level, or higher power, you might say. Since 2001, the lack of competition has tarnished pro wrestling storylines and for that we mourn. Think about it: Katie Vick would've never been born had WCW never died.

The 1990s decade will, no doubt, stand out when wrestling historians and connoisseurs look back decades from now. It was during this period that WWE took a stand and decided to derail the 'Lex Express' and begin to make the transition from the Doink to the Attitude era. Gone were the dark days that featured the likes of 'The Goon' and the Duke 'The Dumpster' Droeses of the world. The Attitude era ushered in stars such as Mankind (one of three Mick Foley alter-egos), De-Generation X (years before WWE would whore out glow sticks to 8-year-old boys) and, of course, The Rock and 'Stone Cold' Steve Austin (before they took the Suburban Commando route and hit the road for Hollywood). Of course, on the other side of the tracks you had WCW, which was pushing the envelope, so to speak, and waging an all-out Monday Night War led by a

THE LOOSE

goody two-shoes turned bad-ass heel in 'Hollywood' Hulk Hogan and his bad guy faction the nWo.

Out of this glorious and unforgettable time came one of the most controversial characters in the history of pro wrestling: Brian Pillman, or perhaps he is better known by his moniker 'The Loose Cannon'. The character that Pillman portrayed was as real as real can get in a business that is based on over-the-top yet scripted storylines. His unpredictable persona saw him do 'worked shoots' that so bordered on the line of insanity, that even the wrestlers themselves believed he was a legitimate nutcase.

'Flyin'' Brian Pillman, as he was dubbed for his high-flying ring ability in his early days wrestling in Canada's famous Stampede Wrestling promotion, began his professional athletic career as a football player where he briefly made a stint with the NFL's Cincinnati Bengals (during the pre-Ickey Shuffle Days).

After a brief run, Pillman eventually left Canada and headed back to the states to wrestle under the NWA banner. It was here that he crafted his skill as one of the first American-born pro wrestlers beside Tom Zenk (The Z-Man, really!?!) to incorporate Mexico's Lucha Libre style of wrestling. Pillman's greatest success in his early NWA-turned-WCW days came when he teamed up with the then Stunning Steve Austin and formed The Hollywood Blonds. He really began to make waves when he joined up with Ric

Flair and the Four Horsemen where he would go on to defeat Japanese legend Jushin 'Thunder' Liger in the very first match in Monday Night Nitro history.

It was around this time that the Loose Cannon's unpredictable behaviour shined and set off a slew of moments on live television that bordered between both fact and fiction. His final straw in WCW was the moment he outed Kevin Sullivan as booker during an 'I Quit' Match on PPV. Pillman was let go by WCW and would find even more infamy in the form of ECW (Extreme Championship Wrestling).

ECW, naturally, was a wrestling fan's third option during the glory days of the Monday Night Wars. It was a hardcore alternative where Pillman shined with his often offbeat behaviour and for being one of the best performers on the mic. (Yes, it's true he once threatened to yank it out and urinate on the fine folks in the ECW Arena.)

Pillman was the talk of the town, and upon entering the WWE, he was well on his way to becoming the talk of all three major players in the game. It was here where he formed an allegiance with some of his former Stampede pals and became a member of the Hart Foundation. It was around this time when he began a programme with his former Hollywood Blond partner Steve Austin and made history by infamously becoming the first and only person to ever pull out a gun during a live televised wrestling event.

Not one to shy away from controversy, Pillman, who was already well on his way to becoming one of wrestling's most highly-talked-about in- and out-of-ring performers, was found dead at the age of 35 the night before a WWE PPV event in which he was supposed to participate. Pillman, who passed away from an undetected heart condition, was well on his way to becoming one of WWE's major players. One can only imagine the impact his career would have had among the annals of WWE contemporaries such as Bret 'Hitman' Hart and Shawn Michaels. Some 13 years after his passing Pillman is still among the most talked about grapplers of his generation and it's safe to say that he had at least one great main event championship run in his sights. The Rogue Horseman who once traded missile drop kicks for F-bombs may be gone, but his influence and mark on pro wrestling will never be forgotten.

Public displays of humiliation, most notably in the form of reluctant haircuts, have been synonymous with professional wrestling for years, dating back to the Golden Age of the 1940s and 50s when attention was focused on the flamboyant exploits of Gorgeous George. 'The Glamour Boy' garnered media buzz for his charismatic character as well as his outlandish gimmickry that revolutionised the industry. However, in one of the 'Human Orchid's' most memorable matches against one of his most noted rivals, fans were treated to a spectacular spectacle that has now become a time-honoured tradition within the annals of professional wrestling. On March 12, 1959, 'Whipper' Billy Watson defeated Gorgeous George in front of 20,000 fans that packed Toronto's Maple Leaf Gardens. Millions also tuned in on television to witness George not only lose the match but to watch his iconic golden-locked head get shaved bald in the face of defeat.

Which brings us to 1986, when Brooklyn-born diminutive pro wrestler Raymond Kessler was thrust into the squared circle spotlight in the form of a friendship with tough guy actor turned pro wrestling personality Mr T. Known best by his nickname the Haiti Kid, the pint-sized superstar grappled with the likes of Sky Low Low and the Lord Littlebrooks of the world, but it was his budding relationship with the former BA Baracus that catapulted him into the main event spotlight of the World

HAIR TODAY GONE TOMORROW

THE LEGEND OF THE HAITI KID

photo:Wrealano@aol.com

20

Wrestling Federation (WWE). Mr T, at the time, was one of Hollywood's brightest stars as everything he seemed to touch turned brighter than the trademark gold wrapped around his neck. Whether it was his role as Clubber Lang in *Rocky III*, his television success on *The A-Team*, or as a cartoon version of himself in which he was portrayed as the owner of a gym that trained mystery-solving gymnasts. Mr T even had his own cereal but 'pity the fool' that thought they tasted better than a bowl of Frosted Flakes.

On that note, not everyone was a fan of his foray into the wrestling business. One wrestler in particular just happened to be the top heel in the company, 'Rowdy' Roddy Piper. Toiling with real-life hatred between the two, WWE continued their feud from the inaugural WrestleMania, and spilled it into the next year's premiere event in the form of a ridiculous boxing match. Despite the star power of legendary boxing trainer Lou Duva and former heavyweight champion 'Smokin' Joe Frazier, it was the presence of the Haiti Kid in Mr T's corner at WrestleMania II that will be remembered most. In the days before TiVo and DVRs, one would have to rewind their VCR tape in order to play back a crucial moment, so let us turn back the clock to an episode of 'Piper's Pit' in the spring of 1986 and recall one of the most outrageous moments in pro wrestling history, one by the way which includes an aging star known as Mae Young giving birth to a hand. In a crude and despicable act, Roddy Piper took cheap heat to a new level when he and his bodyguard (why do wrestlers need bodyguards anyway? Guess that is a different question for another book) 'Cowboy' Bob Orton, kidnapped the Haiti Kid after a match,

tied him to a steel chair and continued to shave his head, Mr T style, on the 'Piper's Pit' set despite the Kid's desperate screams for help.

Obviously Kessler's acting was rewarded with an appearance at that year's Mania, as his reluctant and embarrassing buzz goes down as one of the most memorable of all time. Thankfully for Mr T's only friend in spandex not named Hulk Hogan, he was invited back once again to compete at WrestleMania III in a mixed tag team match with Little Beaver and Hillbilly Jim against Lord Littlebrook, Little Tokyo and King Kong Bundy.

Ironically, Piper would appear on the same historic card as he baby-faced his way to his first of many wrestling 'retirements', but more importantly, his exit from the WWE helped clear the path for Brutus Beefcake, another bad guy turned goody-two-shoes, to snip his way into the hearts of adoring fans by embarrassing 'Adorable' Adrian Adonis with a publicly-watched hair-clipping of his own in front of over 93,000 fans. Since that historic pay-per-view and the immediate success of 'The Barber' gimmick, wrestling fans can never get enough of a little public humiliation. Whether it is at the hands of a hated villain or a lovable character such as the Haiti Kid, everyone, especially hardcore wrestling fans, love watching the weekly train wreck of emotions and mayhem that come with the show.

Sadly, on May 5, 2001, Kessler passed away. However, despite his small size it was his biggest contribution that he will be remembered for most of all. For every time a humiliated star is forced to have his head shaved we cannot help but remember the fighting spirit and legend of the Haiti Kid.

AWESOME:
MIKE AWESOME

photo:Wrealano@aol.com

THE RISE AND FALL OF THE FAT CHICK THRILLA

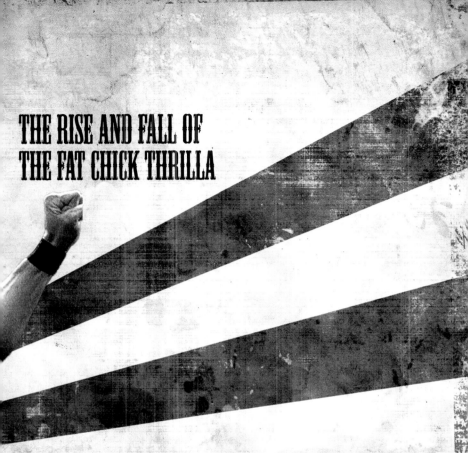

Before he became a household name in the land of Extreme, Mike Alfonso was making a name for himself overseas for Frontier Martial-Arts Wrestling (FMW) as The Gladiator. As he jumped around between Japan and Philadelphia, it would be ten years since his debut in 1989 that Mike Awesome would Awesome Splash his way into the hardcore world of Extreme Championship Wrestling. They say the third time is a charm and upon his arrival for his third stint in ECW, Mike Awesome shocked the loyal fan base and the world by winning the ECW World Heavyweight Championship in a three-way dance against the reigning

champion Tazz (who was on his way to WWE) and his arch-rival, dating back to his FMW days, Masato Tanaka. Despite his simple black trunks and silly mullet hairstyle which easily could have landed him a role as a third member of the Rock n' Roll Express, Awesome destroyed his opponents using an arsenal of moves, some that would make a cruiserweight jealous and some such as the Awesome Bomb, where he would take a helpless opponent and throw him over the top rope and through a table, that made him a major force in ECW.

In spring 2000, the '300 Pound Luchador' made yet another shocking appearance, this time on a much larger scale, attacking Kevin Nash during WCW *Monday Nitro*. His assault on 'Big Sexy' was certainly not the surprise, but the fact that he was still the reigning ECW World Champion certainly was. After refusing to re-sign with ECW, the high-flying big man was set to make his mark for Ted Turner's World Championship Wrestling.

On April 13, 2000, Awesome made wrestling history in the most indescribable way. The ECW World Champion and WCW employee dropped the title to Tazz, who at the

to his immediate push for a globally-recognised wrestling promotion was at an all-time high – that is, until WCW labelled him with the proverbial 'American Dream' polka-dots and started billing him as 'The Fat Chick Thrilla', a gimmick focused less on wrestling talent and more on his lust for heavy-set women.

Awesome's in-ring abilities were unmatched for a big man so it's simply unforgivable that his foray on to the big stage was shrouded in so many lame wrestling personas such as the uncritically-acclaimed answer to the 'Fat

AWESOME:

time was employed by WWE at an ECW event. It would be the first and only time during the heyday of the Monday Night Wars that a WWE guy would face a WCW guy and ironically it was for the ECW title.

Upon entering WCW, Awesome was thrust into the ill-fated New Blood vs. Millionaire's Club squabble that resulted in feuds with Hulk Hogan (who traded in his trademark red and yellow for his not-so-merchandisable F.U.N.B. attire), as well as Diamond Dallas Page. Within a month of his debut in WCW, it would be after an incident in which he tossed Chris Kanyon from a cage that he adopted his often-imitated 'Career Killer' persona (i.e. Randy Orton, Chris Jericho).

The rise of Mike Awesome from his days in Japan as The Gladiator

Chick Thrilla' disaster, 'That 70s Guy'.

An obvious reference to the hit series *That 70s Show*, Awesome appeared on WCW's *Thursday Thunder* programme, the least-watched wrestling show this side of WWE's *Sunday Night Heat*, clad in clothing inspired by the 1970s disco craze. Knee-deep in 'Lava Lamp Lounge' interview segments, it was the occasional hardcore brawls such as a double power bomb atop a *Partridge Family*-inspired bus against the Insane Clown Posse that set Mike Awesome apart from the comical miscues that were being fired throughout the last remaining months of WCW. In the beginning of 2001, Awesome traded in the bell-bottoms for the maple leaf in favour of a run with Team Canada, comprised of Lance Storm, Elix Skipper and a cleanly-shaven and repackaged 'Hacksaw' Jim Duggan. Sadly, his last big moment in the spotlight was having his mullet chopped after losing a Hair vs. Hair match against an already bald Konnan.

A few months later Awesome was thrust into 'The Invasion' storyline that was based on the real-life purchase of WCW by the WWE. In fact, on June 25, 2001, Awesome became the first 'WCW invader' to win gold in WWE when he took advantage of the 24/7 rule and pinned a newly-crowned Rhyno for the now-defunct WWE Hardcore Championship.

After his departure from WWE in 2002, Awesome toiled in the independent wrestling scene for a few years until his appearance at 2005's ECW One Night Stand reunion pay-per-view. Once again it was Mike Awesome that stole the show with his unique combination of hard-hitting, high-flying mayhem. Despite ECW staple Joey Styles referring to him as 'Judas' and the unwelcoming treatment he received from the opening bell, Awesome, along with Masato Tanaka, left the Hammerstein Ballroom that night backed by the legions of ECW faithful rightfully chanting 'This Match Rules'.

Mike Alfonso retired from pro wrestling in 2006, leaving behind a legacy of unforgettable moments as well as some less than memorable gimmicks and although he left wrestling fans much too soon, his comeback at One Night Stand made us all forget the 'Fat Chick Thrilla' and remember just how awesome Mike Awesome truly was.

10 SIDESLAMMERS

TEN BIG MEN NOT AS AWESOME AS MIKE AWESOME

1. 911
2. Giant Gonzales
3. The Yeti
4. Great Khali
5. Big Vito
6. Waylon Mercy
7. Scott 'Flash' Norton
8. Van Hammer
9. Man Mountain Rock
10. Evad Sullivan

TEN WRESTLERS WHO WOULD'VE MADE BETTER STALKERS OF UNDERTAKER'S WIFE THAN DDP

1. Kane
2. Mick Foley
3. Kurt Angle
4. Scott Hall
5. Rick Steiner
6. The Artist Known as Prince Iaukea
7. Rowdy Roddy Piper
8. Saturn
9. Eddie Guerrero
10. Pete Rose

photo Wrealano@aol.com

In 1988 the Atlanta Hawks selected Jorge Gonzalez in the third round of the NBA draft. He was supposed to battle the boards with the likes of basketball gods Hakeem Olajuwon and Moses Malone; instead he was deemed unable to adapt to the daily grind and physical style of the National Basketball Association and thus a bright future in the wrestling business was born. Well, maybe more like a dimly lit bulb, but a future nonetheless. Two years after being chosen by the Hawks, the 7ft 7in giant was offered a job by Ted

EL GIGANTE:

NO WONDER THE NINTH BLUNDER

Turner's WCW. On May 19, 1990, just under two months after WWE's record-breaking WrestleMania VI 'Ultimate Challenge' between the immortal Hulk Hogan and the enormously popular Ultimate Warrior, WCW fired back with a pay-per-view of its own called Capitol Combat. The PPV extravaganza that emanated from Washington DC featured an all-time low for the business as Sting was rescued from an attack by the Four Horsemen by none other than Robocop himself, as well as an all-time high (well, sort of) in the form of an Argentinean giant known simply as 'El Gigante'.

The promotional crossover flop with *Robocop 2* was one thing but not many people had predicted that Gigante's presence in WCW would impact wrestling, much like Firebreaker Chip and the rest of his 'WCW Special Forces' mid-card dwelling faction. A lop-sided feud with World Champion Ric Flair aside, the one-dimensional giant also appeared in the ill-fated Chamber of Horrors match during 1991's Halloween Havoc. From the same company that brought us such mishaps as Fake Sting, the Shockmaster and a Disco Inferno push, it was an accidental pulling of the switch by Cactus Jack that saw Abdullah The Butcher 'fry' in the electric chair. As Abdullah 'fizzled' so did Gigante's tenure in WCW.

In January of 1993, with an infamous bad-guy beard in tow and full body suit complete with airbrushed muscles and hair, 'Giant Gonzales' made his WWE debut, eliminating the Undertaker at the Royal Rumble. With the staying power of a George 'The Animal' Steele Mine doll, Giant Gonzales' brief and unforgettable trip through WWE was only highlighted by a WrestleMania IX loss to the vengeful Undertaker. Yet another big disappointment that could not fill the void left by Andre the Giant, Giant Gonzales will be remembered most for his ridiculous wardrobe that channels the likes of both Men On A

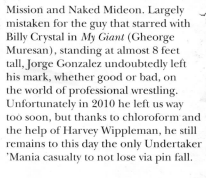

photo:Wrealano@aol.com

Mission and Naked Mideon. Largely mistaken for the guy that starred with Billy Crystal in *My Giant* (Gheorge Muresan), standing at almost 8 feet tall, Jorge Gonzalez undoubtedly left his mark, whether good or bad, on the world of professional wrestling. Unfortunately in 2010 he left us way too soon, but thanks to chloroform and the help of Harvey Wippleman, he still remains to this day the only Undertaker 'Mania casualty to not lose via pin fall.

SIDESLAMMERS

FIVE THINGS THAT MADE US GO HMMMMM.....

1. Spirit Squad
2. G.I. Bro
3. 3-Count
4. Katie Vick
5. Big Vito in a dress

POWER AND ALL THE GLORY

In a lot of ways, Bobby 'The Brain' Heenan had the Midas touch in the World Wrestling Federation. Every wrestler he managed, it seemed, turned into pure wrestling gold once he stood by their side – every wrestler not named Red Rooster, anyway. Hercules Hernandez, whose real name was Raymond Fernandez, was one such wrestler to capitalise on having 'The Weasel' in his corner.

In the mid-1980s, after bouncing around different wrestling factions, usually with a mask on and a belt of some sort around his waist, Hernandez made the move to the World Wrestling Federation and was managed by 'Classy' Freddie Blassie. While he served as a fairly decent heel under that pencil-neck geek, the bearded muscleman was often on the losing end of a match. Case in point: his debut in WrestleMania II saw him fall to Ricky 'The Dragon' Steamboat. The brick house-built wrestler's luck would change, however, after being 'sold' to Heenan shortly thereafter.

Under the tutelage of 'The Brain', Hernandez shed his fake surname, gained some muscle mass, and was reborn as 'Hercules' – a man far more appealing and far less cheesy than

Kevin Sorbo. With steel chains around his neck, which he usually swung at opponents, Hercules became a solid heel in the WWF, and a mainstay in WrestleManias for years to come. Unfortunately so was Koko B. Ware, but we digress.

Some of the bearded wonder's highlights included a long-standing feud with fellow full-nelson finisher Billy Jack Haynes, who he defeated in bloody fashion at WrestleMania III thanks to Heenan's interference. Other highlights included a tug of war with notorious incoherent superstar Ultimate Warrior, and a match against 'The Immortal' Hulk Hogan during a taping of *Saturday Night's Main Event*. Hercules lost that match, but put the Hulkster in his signature backbreaker, which we're guessing would've hurt had wrestling outcomes not been fake.

By the late 1980s, Hercules' hold on TV exposure started to fade. After turning face following his sale from Heenan to the 'Million Dollar Man' Ted DiBiase, he was relegated to squash matches against big men like Earthquake and in 1990, he teamed with Paul Roma as one half of the less than powerful Power and Glory, managed by Slick. The tandem did

photo:Wrealano@aol.com

manage to beat the Rockers in 1990's SummerSlam, but it was clear Hercules' career was heading more toward a Marty Jannetty outcome than a Shawn Michaels one.

Hercules eventually left WWF for WCW and enjoyed some mild success under a mask as the Super Invader, managed by former foe Harley Race. Eventually, he went on to wrestle in New Japan Pro Wrestling, where he grappled once again as Hercules Hernandez.

Raymond Fernandez died in 2004 due to heart complications. While he never won any gold in the WWF, he was a solid, reliable mid-carder who held his own against some of the greatest big men in the business. One thing's for sure: he was far more convincing as a heel than Arnold Schwarzenegger was as an actor in the 1969 dud *Hercules in New York*.

photo:Wrealano@aol.com

SHOW (WITHIN A SHOW) BUSINESS

Often imitated, never duplicated. That's a term often used by wrestlers referring to themselves in first person. Well, if ever that term applied to a wrestler, it was 'Rowdy' Roddy Piper – a complete original who was appealing whether he was blowing smoke at Morton Downey, Jr., was a face, a heel, or somewhere in-between. Arguably best known for his run-ins with Hulk Hogan and partnership with casted-for-no-reason Bob Orton, the wrestler is one of the best and most entertaining ever. And as far as WWE/WWF interview shows or vignettes went, 'Piper's Pit' stands as the most influential and entertaining one by a mile.

The show, which runs now and then for the sake of nostalgia, hit its stride on a regular basis in the mid-1980s, and quickly became the *60 Minutes* of grappling interview segments.

We mourn the good old days of wrestling where 'Piper's Pit' and even copycat segments like Jake 'The Snake' Roberts' 'Snake Pit' and Brutus Beefcake's 'Barbershop' resonated with fans and, more importantly, served as a springboard for a major storyline to start. They also, when executed properly, set up some of the biggest matches of all time.

Some epic contributions of 'Piper's Pit' were Jimmy Snuka getting knocked over the head with a coconut, The Haiti Kid getting kidnapped and given a Mohawk, and in arguably the biggest heel turn of all time, Andre the Giant aligning himself with Bobby 'The Brain' Heenan, ripping off Hulk Hogan's cross, and challenging the 'Immortal' one to a match at WrestleMania III. There are so many more examples of groundbreaking 'episodes', but we'll throw this out because it literally came out of left field… and the closet: Adrian Adonis launching 'The Flower Shop' after a gimmick and life-changing Pit appearance.

As we alluded to before, 'Piper's Pit' was so successful that the WWE (then WWF) tried to catch more lightning in a bottle with similar segments throughout the 1980s and early 1990s and often succeeded on sheer cheesiness alone (we're talking to you, Brother Love). But ever since that decade, the wrestling world's show within a show gimmick went stale and its intention became muddied. It seems nowadays, anyone can get their own 'show' and they've been as appealing as watching Mean Gene Okerlund try on a singlet. If you don't believe us, Google shows hosted by Carlito or MVP.

To his credit, Chris Jericho evoked 'Piper's Pit' with his early 2000s 'Highlight Reel', but it eventually ran its course, and failed to match our favourite kilted superstar's reliable emcee duties. Real men wear kilts.

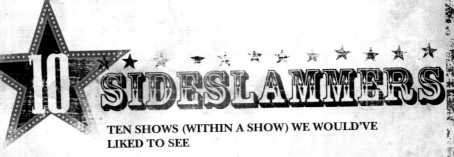

10 SIDESLAMMERS

TEN SHOWS (WITHIN A SHOW) WE WOULD'VE LIKED TO SEE

1. Typhoon's Love Boat
2. The Iron Sheik's Turkish Bathhouse
3. Howard Finkel's House of Tinkle
4. Scott Hall's Celebrity Rehab
5. JYD's Junkyard
6. Glacier's Ice, Ice Baby Carriage
7. Rick Rude's Mustache Ride
8. Hit the Showers with Virgil
9. SD Jones' Post Office
10. You're Welcome with Perry Saturn

MISS ELIZABETH:

BEAUTY AND THE WRESTLING BEASTS

For the majority of us that grew up during the 1980s heyday of Hulkamania and were thrust into the wrestling craze that quickly became a part of pop culture Americana, then it is safe to say that the first protruding bulge in your pants was probably the result of the lovely and incomparable Miss Elizabeth. On August 24, 1985, years before Bam Bam Bigelow would shock the wrestling world by choosing Sir Oliver Humperdink as his manager, 'Macho Man' Randy Savage made headlines of his own by selecting the unknown bombshell simply known as 'Elizabeth' to be his new manager.

Although she was brought into the WWE as part of an angle in which Savage was being courted by several of the federation's biggest-named managers, it came as no surprise that the 'Macho Man' was indeed married to the gorgeous Elizabeth Hulette in real life. For many years Elizabeth stood by the 'Madness' playing a part in major storylines between Savage and superstars such as George 'The Animal' Steele and Ricky 'The Dragon' Steamboat.

photo:Wrealano@aol.com

Perhaps her greatest on-air role was during an episode of *Saturday Night's Main Event* when she enlisted the services of Hulk Hogan in order to protect her man from the evil clutches of the Honky Tonk Man and the Hart Foundation. Elizabeth's decision to persuade the red and yellow to rescue Savage resulted in the formation of the Mega Powers, arguably the most powerful force in wrestling of all time. Of course we would not have taken this team as seriously if they had replaced the 'Mega Power' handshake with the 'Dead Fish' handshake. Even the inaugural SummerSlam back in 1988 was fuelled by the highly popular manager as the main event between the Mega Powers and the Mega Bucks (Andre the Giant and Ted DiBiase) centred on Elizabeth and the 'secret weapon'. Much to the delight of fans, Elizabeth tore off her skirt to reveal red bikini bottoms that single-handedly distracted the Mega Bucks enough to seal a victory for Hogan and Savage, much to the chagrin of Special Referee Jesse 'The Body' Ventura.

Following the epic win, tension soon rose between the Macho Man and the Hulkster, culminating in a WrestleMania V match between the jealous champion and the 24-inch-pythoned challenger. As Hulk Hogan captured the title, Sensational Sherri soon replaced Elizabeth, who had seemingly remained 'neutral' during the Mega Powers explosion.

Occasional appearances aside, Elizabeth would not turn up again until WrestleMania VII, during the conclusion of the Ultimate Warrior–Macho King Retirement Match. As Queen Sherri belittled the fallen king for losing the match, it was Liz who came to his defence to help assure that the heel-to-baby-face-transition would go off smoothly.

The culmination of Elizabeth's reign as the unofficial 'First Lady of Pro Wrestling' was during the on-air engagement and wedding between wrestling's greatest couple, billed appropriately as 'The Match Made In Heaven'. Elizabeth eventually left the WWE and followed Savage to WCW, where she spent the next several years as manager for both the Four Horsemen and the New World Order (nWo) and was even a member of the short-lived trio with Ric Flair and Lex Luger known as Team Package.

After passing in 2003, Elizabeth still remains as one of the most recognised female stars to ever be in the ring. With her body-slamming good looks and unforgettable charm, it is safe to say that Miss Elizabeth helped bridge the gap between yesterday's Fabulous Moolahs and today's Divas and Knockouts.

SPECIAL DELIVERY JONES

AND THE RAIDER OF THE LOST MATCH

If you mention the name Conrad Efraim to wrestling fans, chances are you will get a look more perplexing than having to sit through a Vince McMahon limo explosion a few years back. Efraim, whose wrestling career spanned over 20 years, is perhaps better known by his wrestling persona S.D. 'Special Delivery' Jones. Trained by the 'Unpredictable' Johnny Rodz, the popular performing mainstay was indeed pro wrestling's premier jobber during the WWE's rise to national fame; take that, 'Iron' Mike Sharpe.

Unfortunately for Jones, special delivery and losing go hand in hand and thus the mid-card-dwelling superstar holds the distinct honour of being on the wrong side of one of the most lop-sided matches in WrestleMania history, losing to King Kong Bundy in just 9 seconds during 1985's inaugural event. Synonymous with the 3-count much

like perennial jabronis A.J. Petruzzi and Tiger Chung Lee, S.D. was also Andre the Giant's tag team partner on the night the Eighth Wonder of the World got his hair cut by Big John Studd and Ken Patera. Thankfully for Jones, Bundy did not demand a 5-count during his record breaking 'Mania moment, and thankfully for fans nationwide, LJN created the first and only Special Delivery Jones action figure ever made as part of their successfully collectible Wrestling Superstars toy line. The journeyman wrestler never reached Saturday morning animation status as part of Hulk Hogan's *Rock 'n' Wrestling* cartoon but he did appear in WWE's music video for 'Land of a Thousand Dances', just one of the many hits from 'The Wrestling Album'.

Two years before his untimely death, the Antiguan native made his final WWE appearance, inducting friend and tag team partner Tony Atlas into the Hall of Fame during 'Mania weekend festivities in 2006. His hard work putting over the company's top heels during the Hogan era, along with being immortalised in the non-articulated 8-inch rubber form, will ensure that Jones will go down as one of the industry's most well-respected stars, despite spending the majority of his matches laying flat on his back staring at the lights.

34

For 30 years big Stan Frazier entertained the masses that came to see him wrestle throughout the South Eastern United States. Upon being discovered by Jerry 'The King' Lawler, Frazier's greatest contribution to the sports-entertainment industry was that of a simple-minded, pig-raising country bumpkin by the name of Uncle Elmer. During the mid-80s Frazier was brought into the WWE and joined the wrestling circus as part of The Hillbillies, led by the hugely popular but injured Hillbilly Jim and also featuring 'family members' Cousin Junior and Cousin Luke.

Country Boy' played and continues to resonate with us to this very day. Much like Brakkus and Abe 'Knuckleball' Schwartz, the square-dancing superstar's stint in WWE was brief yet it was his star-studded wedding that will go down as one of the more touching moments in professional wrestling. With a reception that included a poem by Leapin' Lanny Poffo, an appearance by Tiny Tim and a cake in the face to Jesse Ventura, only wrestling's favourite 'Uncle' (sorry, Zebekiah) can claim publicly that he had both Andre the Giant and Hulk Hogan as part of his wedding party.

ELMER THUD

Towering at over 6ft 10in and over 450lb, the former Plowboy Frazier's one-year run as Hillbilly Jim's 'Uncle' will be remembered not so much for his WrestleMania II job on the 'Adorable' Adrian Adonis, but for his unforgettable and nationally-televised in-ring wedding to his real-life wife Joyce, seen during an episode of *Saturday Night's Main Event*.

Clad in his larger-than-life overalls, Elmer helped the rest of the lovable Hillbillies in battling the likes of 'Cowboy' Bob Orton, Big John Studd and Mr Fuji, all the while being adored by smiling fans everywhere as the sweet sounds of Hillbilly Jim's 'Don't Go Messin' With A

photo:Wrealano@aol.com

A HEEL IN THE CROWD

As natural disaster and weather-related gimmicks go in wrestling, they're usually partly cloudy with a chance of really not working. For every successful one like 'The Hurricane', there are about a baker's dozen of 'Glaciers' waiting to limp to their 15-minute mark. In a battle of far-from-epic proportions, John 'Earthquake' Tenta handily wins the contest of 'name based on a Mother Nature screwjob'. A 400-pound-plus wrestler who once squashed a snake with his body (how many people can say that?), Earthquake was as reliable a heel as you could get in the late 1980s and early 1990s in the then-WWF universe. Surprisingly mobile for a big man, he rumbled with the best of the business from Hulk Hogan to Jake 'The Snake' Roberts and was a mainstay in WrestleMania matches for years – winning most of them.

Tenta seemed destined to be in the WWF from an early age when he competed in wrestling competitions. In his teens, he competed and did quite well in the World Junior Wrestling

10 SIDESLAMMERS

TEN WRESTLERS WHO FELL AFTER BEING 'PUSHED'

1. Nathan Jones
2. Bobby Lashley
3. The Great Khali
4. Danny Davis
5. A-Train
6. The Godfather
7. Ken Patera
8. The Mountie
9. Tank Abbott
10. Marc Mero

Championships in Vancouver, and later wrestled in college. Eventually, he moved to Japan and pursued a sumo career but despite finding success, channelling his inner Yokozuna proved not to be his calling.

By the mid-to-late 1980s, Tenta was in the squared circle with tights replacing his sumo diaper. His success in New Japan Wrestling led to his joining the WWF in 1989. The big man made his television debut posing as a fan in the audience during a test-of-strength challenge between Dino Bravo and The Ultimate Warrior. Orchestrated by Bravo's manager Jimmy Hart, the 'Mouth of the South' picked Tenta – dressed in street clothes and looking 40 even though he was really 30 – to sit on the backs of both wrestlers as they did push-ups. Tenta sat on Bravo's back, but delivered a splash on the Warrior when he got down on all fours. The tandem of Tenta and Bravo led to Tenta being known as 'The Canadian Earthquake'. Making his mark in WWF faster than a Rey Mysterio 619, Earthquake earned a match at WrestleMania VI against Hercules and won. That victory propelled Earthquake to main heel status. Throughout his run, he dominated opponents – sending most off on a stretcher – and feuded with the likes of Hulk Hogan, Greg Valentine, and Roberts.

By the early 1990s, Earthquake was pushed to the mid-card level but gained some gold when he formed a tag team with the artist formerly known as Tugboat: Typhoon. Managed by the Mouth of the South, the duo known as The Natural Disasters won the Tag Team Championship but eventually fizzled out when Hart left them and they turned face.

In 1993, Tenta left WWF for Japan, but came back a year later to win yet another WrestleMania match against combustible scrub Adam Bomb

After that squash match, Earthquake was relegated to gimmick matches including a sumo bout against Yokozuna. An injury followed by a money dispute led Tenta to leave WWF for WCW in 1994. He wrestled under the name Avalanche for a while, but was forced to change it to The Shark. He never gained the success he had at the WWF in WCW and would eventually come back to his WWF roots in 1998, wrestling under a mask as one of the 'Oddities'. (His weight loss prevented him from returning as Earthquake, supposedly.) That lame gimmick was short-lived. Sadly, Tenta was forced to retire in 2004 after being diagnosed with an incurable form of bladder cancer. He died on June 7, 2006. The last time he appeared on WWE TV was fittingly as Earthquake during the classic 20-Man Gimmick Battle Royal. No snakes were harmed that evening.

photo: Wrestlanofiand.com

photo:Wrealano@aol.com

One major trend that clearly worked in the 1980s and no other decade in the then-WWF Universe was wrestlers being escorted to the ring by four-legged animals or reptiles instead of managers. Whereas skanky chicks with fake boob managers were all the rage in the 1990s and early 2000s, pets reigned in the WWF. It's hard to mention Koko B. Ware without thinking of his parrot pal Frankie by his side. Would the character have been as effective had he not had that macaw with him as he flapped his arms like a bird and danced awkwardly on his way to the ring? We say not. We'd also suggest that Frankie kept our attention off Ware's worst character flaw: a painfully bright outfit and sunglasses that even Kanye West wouldn't wear.

You could get away with a lot of things in the 1980s: bad hair, terrible fashion and cheesy music. That notion played out throughout pop culture and the World Wrestling Federation was among the biggest offenders. Take one look at Rick Rude's hair, and you know instantly what decade he rose to prominence in. Watch any promo with or without Mean Gene Okerlund, and the graphics will tell you right away that it was the Ronald Reagan era. Google 'Strike Force' and 'Girls in Cars' and you'll see some quintessential MTV-friendly cheese.

Frankie wasn't alone in the jungle that was WWF in the 1980s. If Dr Doolittle could talk to the WWF animals, he'd probably strike up a great conversation with Matilda. The British Bulldogs were an already appealing

WE'LL MAKE GREAT PETS

photo:Wrealano@aol.com

tag team, but when they brought an actual bulldog to lead them to the ring, they reached a different level. Who doesn't remember watching the tandem escorted to the ring by the stone-faced portly dog? We're pretty sure on numerous occasions Davey Boy Smith and the Dynamite Kid dressed her up in an outfit to match them, and the amazing thing was it wasn't degrading to anyone involved. We're also pretty sure camera crews gave Matilda more close-ups on WWF than Miss Elizabeth during her impressive run, which included a pivotal dognapping case involving The Islanders. Not cool, Haku.

Whereas Matilda was a calming presence to wrestling fans, Jake 'The Snake' Roberts' pet Damien made everyone feel a little more uneasy. Following each match, Roberts would unload his pet snake from a sack, and let him squirm on his defeated opponent. (One wonders if Roberts paved the way for *Fear Factor*.) Damien never seemed to do anything other than move around, but one would imagine it feeling sort of

gross to have a snake roaming around your body – especially after a loss. Like Matilda, Damien played a role in various storylines – notably getting squashed by Earthquake during a feud and coming up against Ricky 'The Dragon' Steamboat's own Komodo dragon – which sadly didn't have a name. We think anyway…

Through the years, some animals have appeared on WWF/WWE programming (Al Snow had a Chihuahua but you tried to forget that, didn't you?) but they never played as big a role as the bird, the dog and the snake. One wonders if adding a four-legged friend might have saved some one-dimensional stars that never really took off the way they should have. Who wouldn't have wanted to see Snitsky with a pony or Lex Luger with a llama?

photo:Wrealano@aol.com

6 SIDESLAMMERS

TOP SIX WRESTLING 'PETS'

1. Matilda (British Bulldogs)
2. Damien (Jake The Snake)
3. Frankie (Koko B. Ware)
4. George 'The Animal' Steele
5. Road Warrior Animal
6. Gorilla Monsoon

photo:Wrealano@aol.com

DUMB AND DUMBER:

CRAPPY MOVIE EVEN CRAPPIER GIMMICKS

Obviously if you have gotten this far you must have realised that this book is a homage to pro wrestling gods and gimmicks and not obnoxious Jim Carrey movies. On that note, let's grab a ringside seat and take a closer look at some of the dumbest gimmicks to ever step foot in the squared circle:

ARACHNAMAN

Despite shooting silly string from his wrists and being a complete blatant rip-off of Marvel Comics' Peter Parker was gone from WCW quicker than you can say Earl Robert of Eaton. Speaking of secret identities, the purple and yellow webbed mid-carder who once went toe-to-toe with a then 'Stunning' Steve Austin was actually mild-mannered NWA/WCW mainstay Brad Armstrong. Sadly this was not Brad's only foray into masked wrestling, as he once masqueraded as one-third of the WCW Six-man Tag Team Champions as 'Badstreet' along with fellow Fabulous Freebird members (Michael 'P.S.' Hayes and Jimmy 'Jam' Garvin). Thankfully for Armstrong, despite the fact that his gimmick as a Spider-Man knockoff was so awful, it didn't prevent his dad 'Bullet' Bob from being inducted into the WWE Hall of Fame in 2010.

photo:Wrealano@aol.com

THE DING DONGS

Hailing from 'Bellville, USA', which is probably not from Parts Unknown, this tag team comprised of journeymen jabronis Jim Evans and Richard Sartain clad in full orange bodysuits, complete with masks and obnoxious bells on both their ankles and their wrists. Debuting at Clash of Champions in 1989 against George South and Cougar Jay, The Ding Dongs eventually went the way of the buffalo after getting squashed by The Skyscrapers, leading to one of the greatest calls in wrestling history by a pre-Stetson hat wearing Jim Ross: 'They've unmasked The Ding Dongs! I still don't know who they are and they've been unmasked.'

BEAVER CLEAVAGE

When Headbanger Thrasher went out with a knee injury in May 1999, his tag team partner Mosh (Christopher Warrington) was soon left in wrestling limbo, eventually appearing in black-and-white vignettes as the 'son' of Mrs Cleavage, which was an obvious parody of the *Leave It To Beaver* television show, except this family was knee-deep in sexual innuendos. Ironically, the Cleavage gimmick was not the only one Warrington is unforgettably remembered for. Before they head-banged their way to the top of the WWE tag team world, Mosh and Thrasher were managed by Brother Love and booked on the first ever *Shotgun Saturday Night* WWE programme as The Flying Nuns, Mother Smucker and Sister Angelica.

When the Monday Night War between WCW and WWE ended, one of the instant casualties – aside from competition and overall excitement – was the art of the surprise appearance or run-in. Throughout the late 1990s and early 2000s, both wrestling companies had mastered it – especially WCW. Who could forget Scott Hall walking on camera 'unannounced' and bringing his friend Kevin Nash to the *Nitro* party? Or the time Rick Rude showed up on *Nitro* just hours before he appeared on a taped *Raw is War*?

WrestleMania X8 in Toronto? Of course. Did we care when Shane McMahon started unveiling WCW competitors as part of the 'Invasion' angle? Sorry, Lance Storm, but no. Whereas the Monday Night Wars were all about shocking the audience, the last decade-plus has been all about keeping fans informed of what's to come next. Well, aside from that terrible DDP stalker angle, which surprised as many people as it let down.

To get into this a little deeper, when WCW superstar Goldberg, after years of negotiating, finally came to the WWE in 2003, the company didn't have him

RUN-IN ON EMPTY

Since *Nitro* and eventually *Raw* aired live, there was always an element of the unpredictable each Monday night. When WCW was at its height, you saw WWF wrestlers dropping in to WCW unannounced. When WCW hit the skids, it was exciting to see which WCW wrestler would jump ship to the WWF. Everyone remembers the night Chris Benoit, Dean Malenko and Eddie Guerrero popped up, right?

The surprising ship-jumps unfortunately ended when Vince McMahon purchased WCW in 2000. Sure, surprise appearances and run-ins still happen today but it's so telegraphed now. Case in point: if Alberto Del Rio has the belt, and he's simultaneously feuding with John Cena and CM Punk, one would figure out that one of the three may interfere in a match between two of the three.

WWE started spelling out run-ins and appearances for the audience ever since WCW closed its Atlanta offices. Did we know nWo's Kevin Nash and Scott Hall would try to interfere during the epic Hulk Hogan/The Rock match during

interrupt a match during WrestleMania XIX or debut unannounced. Instead, they ran a promo during the pay-per-view that he was coming to the organisation. On the very next night, Goldberg debuted on *Raw* much to no one's surprise to take on The Rock. The man who used to scream 'You're next!' ended up taking on Dwayne Johnson at a sloppy seconds kind of pay-per-view called Backlash.

Oddly enough, the last time WWE truly had a surprise run-in or cameo was during that aforementioned WrestleMania XIX when Roddy Piper hit Hulk Hogan with a pipe during his street fight against Vince McMahon. Just thinking about that makes us long for the good old days when there was an element of surprise in wrestling. We miss those 'out of the blue' moments. It's time to bring it back. We haven't been legitimately surprised by anything that's gone on in wrestling since Mike Awesome crashed WCW *Monday Nitro* while still ECW champion.

WRESTLER RUN-IN
SHANE DOUGLAS

What's the worst gimmick in wrestling history and why?

Dean Douglas! You take the hottest heel in the biz (in '96) and turn him into an uninteresting character devoid of any voice inflection, etc!? Brilliant Vince!

Did you create your in and out of ring persona? How did it come about?

'The Franchise' evolved out of very loose direction from Paul. In fact, the only REAL direction he gave me was to say this character is the captain of the high school football team that steals everybody and anybody's girlfriend. The rest was created as we went!

Which wrestling death hit you the hardest, and why?

Both Bam Bam's and Candido's hit me right in the gut!!! I LOVED both of them like brothers, so losing them was horrifying for obvious reasons.

Who were your wrestling inspirations growing up?

Bruno Sammartino, obviously and, believe it or not, Dic Flair. Bruno has ALWAYS been a gentleman AND a professional. I have NEVER seen those qualities in Flair! What a letdown to meet him and him fall so far short of what I expected. I go much further into this in my book.

What was the coolest gimmick ever and why?

For me, 'Mr Perfect' because Curt so evoked the image of an athlete combined with the entertainment necessary in wwe (notice the lower case). To me, he personified what a great wrestler, in the new paradigm of entertainment, should be.

Who is/was the best in the business?

Curt, Bret, Owen, Candido, Bam Bam... take your pick!

Was it hard or easy to do so well with mic skills?

Not for me! In fact, I am so amazed that it is becoming such a lost art in wrestling! Where I came from, talking 'smack' was something every **eighth** grader was good at.

Although he captured the AWA World Heavyweight Championship against wrestling great Nick Bockwinkel and held it for over a year, the brash-talking heel persona of Curt Hennig reached new heights when he entered the WWE in 1988 and began calling himself Mr Perfect. Several weeks before his in-ring debut the second-generation star was portrayed as the perfect athlete, hitting half-court basketball shots with ease, bowling a 300, sinking impossible golf putts and even catching his own Hail Mary football pass. (Bet Doug Flutie can't do that?) In fact he even taught MLB Hall of Famer Wade Boggs the 'perfect swing'.

The son of Larry 'The Axe' Hennig first got his big break in the American Wrestling Association, a promotion known best for its weekly *All Star Wrestling* programme on ESPN as well as the unforgettable uncooked turkey on a pole match won by Team Challenge Series hero Jake 'The Milkman' Milliman. The Minnesota native eventually departed Verne Gagne's playground and found a new home in the form of the WWE. Beating the likes of the Red Rooster and Blue Blazer, Hennig's debut was perfect as he remained undefeated for well over a year. Led by 'The Genius' Lanny Poffo, Mr Perfect was even once considered a serious threat to Hulk Hogan's World Championship.

However, his first televised defeat came at the hands of 'The Barber' Brutus Beefcake at WrestleMania VI. Trading in wrestling's resident Frisbee tosser for its most well-known weasel, Hennig soon enlisted the services of Bobby 'The Brain' Heenan. His time as a member of the infamous Heenan Family culminated in one of the greatest Intercontinental title runs of all time. However, it was a broken tailbone and bulging discs that forced this great in-ring performer to drop the gold for good against Bret Hart at SummerSlam in 1991. Plagued by nagging injuries, Hennig still managed to spend the next

PERFECT ATTENDANCE

few years in the spotlight whether as a colour commentator, special guest referee or as Ric Flair's 'executive consultant'.

In 1997 Hennig signed with WCW and once again returned to being one of the best in-ring technicians of his generation. As a member of the Four Horsemen as well as former leader of the West Texas Rednecks, Hennig was never too far from controversy. With a United States title, 'Rap Is Crap' country song and retirement match loss to Buff Bagwell on his résumé, Hennig soon drifted out of the mainstream-wrestling spotlight in the summer of 2000. Two years later, Mr Perfect made a surprise appearance at the Royal Rumble, lasting to the final three and earning a full-time contract with WWE. Hennig solidified a Hall of Fame career by holding his own against the best of the best at the time. Sadly it was a 'plane ride from hell', including a showdown with Brock Lesnar that eventually got Hennig released from his contract. In 2003 Hennig passed away but his legacy now lives on in the form of his son and third-generation wrestling star Joe Hennig, better but strangely known as Michael McGillicutty.

He was sarcastic, pompous, and an asshole, but during a time when it was frowned upon to root for the bad guy, Mr Perfect found a place in the heart of all wrestling fans. Albeit a secret respect and admiration for Hennig's wrestling genius, he was, as only he can say, 'absolutely perfect'.

THE MISSING

Far past the glitz, glamour and spectacle that is professional wrestling and well beyond the cookie sheets and barbwire bats that help solidify its 'anything goes' mentality lies the most outrageous, bizarre and over-the-top characters the world has ever seen. For sure you have heard of the green-tongued George 'The Animal' Steele, whose animalistic tendencies included his appetite for all things turnbuckle, or Abdullah the Butcher, whose penchant for blood usually began and ended with a fork carving to a helpless opponent's forehead, but perhaps among the more perplexing personas ever created was the one created by Dewey Robertson.

After a decent 'face' run throughout many territories in the 1960s and 70s, the Canadian-born grappler changed his look and in 1983 he became The Missing Link. Known more for banging his head into turnbuckles than for his devastating flying headbutt finisher, the Link was one of wrestling's most out-of-control personalities. In fact, a full-page photo of The Missing Link ran in an April 1985 issue of *Sports Illustrated* complete with his trademark green and blue face paint and oddly-shaved head. Although his career on the national

photo:Pete Lederberg

LINK

WWE stage was brief, the insane heel from Parts Unknown undoubtedly left his mark throughout the wrestling universe, disposing of a who's-who of wrestling jobbers during the mid-80s including both 'Quick Draw' Rick McGraw and Salvatore Bellomo.

Lasting in the WWE for about as long as Shawn Michaels did in the 2003 Royal Rumble, The Missing Link continued his wild antics during his time in World Class Championship Wrestling. Despite being controlled by a handler/manager throughout his career in order to tame his wild behaviour, much like the love/hate relationship between the 'Ugandan Giant' Kamala and Kimchee, the wrestling tales of Dewey Robertson were forever chronicled in the 2006 autobiography *Bang Your Head: The Real Story of The Missing Link*. Even today, as insanity reaches an all-time high, there will only be one true missing link of professional wrestling.

WRESTLER RUN-IN
SHANE HELMS

'The Benoit tragedy also hit hard for many reasons, obviously the loss of a friend is always hard but the overall insane details of his last days are just something that's just hard to comprehend. We had become really close in the last two years of his life and during my time away from the ring due to a spinal fusion, out of all my friends, Benoit actually called me the most. Having gone through a similar surgery, he was a constant source of inspiration and advice on how to deal with the injury, and I still recall how grateful I felt that he would take the time to call me. We last spoke on a Thursday night, the very day before he killed his wife. I'll never forget our last phone call, and I'll never forget the complete shock I felt when I heard the details on what all transpired. On one hand he was a great friend and someone everyone in the business that I love looked up to. And on the other hand, he committed monstrous crimes. It's still to this day, something that's hard to think about.'

CRIPPLING A LEGACY

When John Cena and Brock Lesnar debuted in WWE, they did so in response to Vince McMahon's 'Ruthless Aggression' challenge. The chairman came up with the term as a way of trying to motivate wrestlers to make an instant statement in the company. Chris Benoit, who made statements on almost a nightly basis in the business for decades, hilariously sported a shirt in response called 'Toothless Aggression'. The gesture – alluding to the loss of his front incisor – was a rare side of humour from the silent star who always made up for his lack of personality on the mic with unparalleled wrestling skills.

Benoit's story was one that would've made a great movie one day. He idolised wrestlers Bret Hart and the Dynamite Kid, worked in the infamous Hart 'Dungeon' to hone his craft, paid his dues by wrestling all over the world for various companies,

photo:Wrealano@aol.com

and all the while, earned the respect and admiration of his peers and fans alike. The movie would've culminated a few decades later on the night he won the World Wrestling Championship at WrestleMania XX after years of being relegated to mid-card status. It would've been wonderful if the story ended there, but we know it didn't.

The crimes Benoit committed were so heinous that it's hard to remember a time in which he reigned over the wrestling world. WWE has all but erased him from all programming since news broke that he killed his wife, young son and then himself on June 24, 2007. Who can blame them? As spectacular as his wrestling days were, the Rabid Wolverine's actions before taking his own life have tainted his legacy forever. It's hard to look at the up side in what's arguably the biggest tragedy of all time in wrestling, but we'll try to remember Benoit as the wrestling great he was instead of the monster he turned into.

Since he was a kid growing up in Edmonton, Benoit wanted to become a wrestler and worked his ass off for it to become a reality. For the better part of two decades, he bounced around the independent circuit and New Japan Pro Wrestling before landing in WCW (for a brief stay) and ECW. In the latter Paul Heyman company, he earned the nickname 'The Crippler' following a match in which he accidentally broke Sabu's neck and ran with that moniker to reasonable success. He shared the Tag Team Championship with Dean Malenko, and was well on his way to becoming a top heel in the company but his work visa expired, and that was that. Returning to NJPW was actually a blessing for Benoit, who ended up going to WCW since the two organisations had a working relationship together.

With Hulk Hogan, Ric Flair, and other icons in the business in WCW, Benoit found himself usually in the mid-card category. Sure, he'd have memorable feuds (especially with Kevin Sullivan and Booker T), held several titles while there (US Champ among them), and was a member of two versions of the Four Horsemen, but was never really given a chance to shine as a main eventer.

With wrestling spoiler websites going crazy, Benoit left WCW (after winning the Heavyweight Championship) for the WWE with fellow WCW defectors and friends Malenko, Eddie Guerrero, and Perry Saturn in 2000 to form The Radicalz. Within a month, he beat Chris Jericho to win the Intercontinental title. Throughout the next few years, Benoit took part in main event or main event-calibre matches against everyone from Kurt Angle to Stone Cold Steve Austin to Guerrero.

By 2005, Benoit had reached the pinnacle of his career. He won the Royal Rumble after he eliminated the Big Show, and earned a title shot at WrestleMania XX, which he won via a Triple Threat match between himself, Triple H and Shawn Michaels. The PPV memorably ended with he and long-time friend Guerrero celebrating their titles in the ring. For the next two years, Benoit fought off injuries and won additional titles including the US Championship and the ECW World Championship. Stories suggest he was on his way to regaining the latter championship in a pay-per-view at the time of his death.

We're not sure if injuries (he had countless concussions), 'roid rage' or something else caused Benoit to do the unthinkable, but, in the end, it doesn't matter. Two innocent people are dead, and a wrestling legacy he fought so hard to earn has all but vanished.

TINY 'ZEUS'
FROM Z-GANGSTA TO Z-WORST

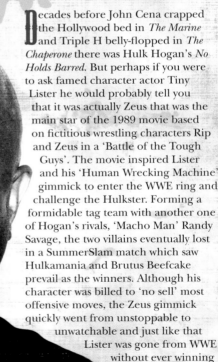

Decades before John Cena crapped the Hollywood bed in *The Marine* and Triple H belly-flopped in *The Chaperone* there was Hulk Hogan's *No Holds Barred.* But perhaps if you were to ask famed character actor Tiny Lister he would probably tell you that it was actually Zeus that was the main star of the 1989 movie based on fictitious wrestling characters Rip and Zeus in a 'Battle of the Tough Guys'. The movie inspired Lister and his 'Human Wrecking Machine' gimmick to enter the WWE ring and challenge the Hulkster. Forming a formidable tag team with another one of Hogan's rivals, 'Macho Man' Randy Savage, the two villains eventually lost in a SummerSlam match which saw Hulkamania and Brutus Beefcake prevail as the winners. Although his character was billed to 'no sell' most offensive moves, the Zeus gimmick quickly went from unstoppable to unwatchable and just like that Lister was gone from WWE without ever winning a single match.

LISTER

GIMMICK EVER

In the mid-90s Lister once again left his regular gig in Tinsel Town for a taste of the wrestling spotlight. Competing this time around as Z-Gangsta, Lister's WCW career was just as unimpressive as his first go round. Just like the immortal one once asked 'What's that smell?' during a climactic scene in *No Holds Barred*, we know this time around it's not 'cocky' but it's the smell of Tiny 'Zeus' Lister's failed wrestling career.

WRESTLER RUN-IN
MATT HYSON
FORMERLY SPIKE DUDLEY, WWE & ECW

'Sometimes the worst gimmicks turn into the best on sheer comedy value. And in the late 80s when the WWF went really gimmick crazy there were plenty of goofy ones. But I think when they had Greg Valentine dye his hair black and tagged him with Honky Tonk Man was probably the hardest for me to take. I liked Honky, he was great at his gimmick. But it was nothing like the Hammer. He was such an awesomely fearful villain. I hated changing his character into a comedy act.'

Only a select few superstars can lay claim to singing their own entrance theme song. For years Shawn Michaels has obnoxiously waltzed down the aisle complete with streamers and confetti to the tune of his trademark 'Sexy Boy' music. These days it is John Cena's rap and not his 'five knuckle shuffle' that is the standard by which all wrestler-related song tunes are measured. There is, however, only one song that connects more with true wrestling fans than any other. That song is 'Grab Them Cakes' by the one and only Junkyard Dog, which featured these immortal lines:

And when you get yourself started it's hard to stop,

You just go for your partner's you know what.

With its catchy lines along with Sylvester Ritter's over-the-top charisma, this song helped build the larger-than-life JYD persona and helped transform him into one of the major players during the WWF's 80s wrestling boom. With his trademark 'Thump' tights and featured role during Hulk Hogan's *Rock 'n' Wrestling* Saturday morning cartoon, the Junkyard Dog quickly became one of the most talked about personalities in the history of pro wrestling. Despite never winning the big one (WWF World Title) or the small one for that matter (WWF Intercontinental Title), Ritter almost always stole the show with help from his in-ring crowd interactions and his signature chain and dog collar.

As the WWF elevated itself into a national powerhouse, JYD was one of the company's brightest stars despite his position among the mid-carders. Ritter's most notable adversaries during these days were a rogues' gallery of WWF villains such as Greg 'The Hammer' Valentine, 'The Outlaw' Ron Bass, 'The King' Harley Race, and the Funk Brothers (Jimmy Jack Funk not

WHO LET THE DOG OUT?

included) in a feud which included the branding of Jimmy Hart on national television. Ritter would soon exit the federation and in a bid to import WWF talent he would resurface in the newly-christened WCW in 1989. Including his part in the goody-two-shoes anti-horsemen stable led by Sting known as the 'Dudes with Attitudes', the Junkyard Dog never again captured the same magic he once had during his WWF days, where he would posthumously be inducted into the Hall of Fame in 2004. Only the hugely popular JYD can get away with lip-synching 'Grab Them Cakes' during the inaugural Slammy Awards.

It can be hair colour for some or athletic ability for others. It can be something as complex as intellect or something as simple as freckles. People always use the phrase 'it runs in the family', and genetics proves that it's a pretty valid statement. Well, Andre the Giant's grandfather was almost 8 feet tall and his parents were over 6 feet. Yes, the wrestling legend's genes created a blueprint for his righteous path.

There has never been a bigger man in the wrestling business – figuratively and literally – than one Andre Rousimoff. The career of the Frenchman, who seemed larger than the Eiffel Tower, around the world. He'd become a household name in the WWF – marketed as the 'Eighth Wonder of the World' – especially when Vince Sr. sold the company to Vince Jr. in 1982.

Andre the Giant was arguably second to Hogan as WWF's most famous 'face' for years, and thanks to a strong supporting role as lovable giant Fezzek in the instant classic *The Princess Bride*, his popularity went well beyond the wrestling ring.

Throughout his run in the WWF, Andre battled health issues, which were explained on television in made-up storylines (seriously, did you believe

WHEN SIZE REALLY MATTERED

plays like one long highlight reel – so much so that every 'big man' who has ever stepped into the ring after he did – from the Big Show to the Great Khali – has had to live up to his size 24 shoes. No one has or will ever come close.

Rousimoff was born in 1946, and learned fairly early on that he wasn't meant for a Hornswoggle kind of life. He was reportedly over 200 pounds and 6 feet tall as an early teen – too big to fit on the cheese bus and likely too big to fit in at all in a school setting. Since he wanted to pursue a career working on a farm anyway, Andre dropped out of school before reaching high school. Thankfully for us his post-school plans led him on a new path in Paris.

After being shown the ropes by wrestlers who were in awe of his large size, Andre took up the squared circle. Wrestling came naturally for the 7-foot-tall giant. Wrestling under the name 'Jean Ferre' in Europe, Africa, Japan, Canada, and other parts unknown, Rousimoff met with Vince McMahon, Sr. and eventually joined the World Wrestling Federation. Renamed Andre the Giant, the larger-than-life grappler was heavily booked in the States and he was scared of King Kong Bundy?). By 1987, his ginormous condition had led to significant back issues that would lead to surgery, but it didn't stop Andre from participating in his biggest storyline ever. In an infamous 'Piper's Pit' telecast, Andre – feeling slighted by Hogan and the company for years of under-the-radar dominance (he'd allegedly never been pinned) – aligned himself with heel manager Bobby 'The Brain' Heenan and challenged Hogan to a heavyweight championship match at WrestleMania III. In one of the most shocking moments in wrestling history, he notoriously ripped the T-shirt and crucifix off the Hulkster.

The WrestleMania III match was arguably the best-promoted and most popular match of all time. Hogan defeated the Giant by body-slamming him and delivering his signature leg drop, but Andre would have his revenge a year later when he won the title under the tutelage of Ted DiBiase. Following that match, which featured 'evil twin' guest referee Earl Hebner, Andre sold the belt to the 'Million Dollar Man'. President Jack Tunney would soon negate that 'deal', but a title is a title.

Following that win and failed purchase, Andre, still battling health issues, continued to dominate as the biggest heel in the business. He feuded with everyone from 'Hacksaw' Jim Duggan to Jake 'The Snake' Roberts, and eventually won the WWF Tag Team title along with Haku (of all people) as the Heenan-run Colossal Connection.

Heenan and Andre would eventually part ways following a Colossal WrestleMania VI loss to Demolition that 'The Brain' blamed on Andre, and for the remainder of his run in the WWF, Andre was back in face form, making sporadic appearances. His last appearance in the WWF was at SummerSlam in 1991 where he helped the Bushwhackers in their win against the Natural Disasters. After his in-ring career in the WWF ended, he made appearances for All Japan Pro Wrestling. On January 27, 1993, he died at 46 of heart failure while in Paris for his father's funeral.

To this day, Andre the Giant remains a celebrated wrestler and pop culture icon. You see his face on those 'Obey' campaigns, you watch him in *The Princess Bride* with your kids or grandkids on Blu-ray, and you read stories about his tenacity and drinking (um, he drank a lot) in just about any biography from a wrestler who knew him. Andre is long gone, but he lives on.

5 SIDESLAMMERS

FIVE REASONS WHY WE STILL LOVE ANDRE THE GIANT EVEN THOUGH HE WAS FRENCH

1. Ken Patera and Big John Studd cut his hair, which translated to a better action figure
2. He bitchslapped Hulk Hogan on 'Piper's Pit'
3. He pranced around in a mask as one of 'the Machines' but fooled no one
4. He sold the belt to Ted DiBiase, because 'everyone has a price.'
5. He was more believable in seven minutes of *The Princess Bride* than John Cena was in an hour and 45 minutes of *The Marine*

BIG
JOHN STUDD:
THE NINTH WONDER OF THE WORLD

Next to Andre the Giant, Big John Studd was the biggest and baddest the WWF threw in the ring in the 1980s. Placing second to the 'Eighth Wonder of the World' isn't a bad consolation prize. Often paired against each other thanks to their large frames, Studd more than held his own against Andre in battles best referred to as 'Goliath vs. Goliath', or perhaps the best example of Gorilla Monsoon's famous line in which 'the irresistible force meets the immovable object.'

'Big' John Minton broke on to the scene wearing a mask as one half of the Masked Executioners with his trainer Killer Kowalski. After winning the WWF Tag Team titles with his mentor and partner in the mid-1970s, he took to the road and competed in various territories under such guises as Captain USA and The Masked Superstar II. Unlike Rey Mysterio, Jr. in the WCW, however, once the mask came off for Studd – it stayed off.

By 1982, the grizzly man was back with the WWF following a run in the NWA and stayed at or close to main event status for years to come. With 'Classy' Freddie Blassie at ringside, Studd made an impact almost immediately, sending opponents home on stretchers and sporting arguably the best long tights of all time (loved those stars!) One of Studd's finest hours was a 'Bodyslam Challenge' in which he offered a five-figure sum to any wrestler who could slam him to the mat. When Andre the Giant accepted the challenge and nearly slammed him (Blassie interceded), a popular feud was born and remained for years.

The most fuel added to the feud came when Studd aligned himself with Bobby 'The Brain' Heenan. Who could forget when Studd, along with Heenan Family member Ken Patera, cut Andre's hair after a match? The answer is no one. Even LJN created a new rubbery Andre figure *sans* the Roseanne Barr hair they gave him in their first incarnation after the haircut!

The Studd and Andre feud became the stuff of legend at WrestleMania I when Andre slammed him during the '$15,000 Body Slam Challenge'. The image of one big man slamming another is etched in our wrestling minds forever. Following that epic slam, Studd partnered with fellow big man King Kong Bundy to wage war against Andre. That said, he did set his sights on William 'The Refrigerator' Perry by the time WrestleMania II came around. After he and the Chicago Bear eliminated each other during that event's 20-man battle royal, Studd spent the better part of the year with Bundy, contending for the tag belts and still hell-bent on being known as the 'true giant' of the WWF. The bearded and bald tandem also waged war against the masked team known as The Machines – one half of that pair was obviously Andre the Giant, having found a loophole at the time after being suspended for not showing up for a match against Big John.

Studd retired in 1986 but briefly came back three years later as a face and reached a career highlight by winning the Royal Rumble. Naturally, he took on Andre once again during his final run. The two men were so inseparable in the 1980s, they even co-starred in a bad Dudley Moore movie together (*Micki & Maude*).

Studd died of liver cancer and Hodgkin's disease on March 20, 1994. He was inducted in the WWE Hall of Fame ten years later and remembered as a 'giant' in the business.

photo:Wrealano@aol.com

WHO'S NEXT!?

Pro wrestling has had its fair share of streaks. Sure the Undertaker streak at WrestleMania is impressive but what about the underrated streaks that have gone on throughout the years such as the yellow streak sprayed down 'Macho Man' Randy Savage's back every other week by the nWo during the late 90s or the streak of *Raw* shows that we have not watched since John Cena became a permanent fixture in the WWE Championship title picture? There is also the never-ending streak of Hall of Fame ceremonies we have to suffer through before Lord Alfred Hayes finally gets the recognition he deserves. You can't forget the awful streak of terrible movies Hulk Hogan made during his late 80s semi-retirement and the bad luck streak that began for WCW soon after Riki Rachtman hosted his first Nitro Party.

On the other hand perhaps is the most overrated streak of all time, the Goldberg streak. Knee deep in a failed football career, Bill Goldberg began his quick climb up the *Nitro* ladder by defeating Hugh Morrus in his debut match on September 22, 1997. His over-hyped push backed by his none-dimensional gimmick of a silent beast with superhuman strength helped Goldberg reach heights quicker than a Santa's Slay home video release. The king of the squash match made his pay-per-view debut by pinning fellow gridiron grappler Steve McMichael. At 74-0 (seriously, how many of those were won against Jerry Flynn on *Thunder*?) Goldberg challenged the then United States Champion Raven and despite interference from the Flock, the former Georgia Bulldog had already captured his first wrestling gold.

As Goldberg began dabbling in the main event scene it was his 'who's next' catchphrase that helped fans notice his expanding winning streak as well as his expanding ego. In just his 108th match, Goldberg jack-hammered his way into the wrestling record books by defeating 'Hollywood' Hulk Hogan for the WCW World Heavyweight Championship. After 174 straight victories Kevin Nash finally snapped the elusive streak, thanks to a stun-gun wielding run-in from Scott Hall. Goldberg's limited in-ring skills were overshadowed by his intimidating and pyro-filled ring entrances. Meanwhile, in the sincerest form of mockery, long-time scrub wrestler Duane Gill was dubbed Gillberg by the WWE and thus a new streak was born complete with sparklers, fire extinguishers and the greatest wrestling parody this side of the Blue World Order.

THE TURNPIKE INCIDENT

Much like the unanswered question of 'why did the chicken cross the road?', wrestling fans for decades have been wondering why their hometown hero 'Hacksaw' Jim Duggan and his arch-enemy the Iron Sheik were arrested together by New Jersey State police on May 26, 1987, while driving from a wrestling show on the New Jersey Turnpike. It was bad enough that the 2x4-wielding tough guy was under the influence of alcohol and marijuana, while the former WWF champion was busted for being in possession of various other drugs. But together in the same car? That, my friends, is preposterous.

Seriously, isn't that like Superman and Lex Luthor getting caught robbing a bank together? Sadly for Duggan he was released while the Iron Sheik received one year's probation; meanwhile, it was a black eye for the wrestling industry that may have single-handedly changed the business forever, because since that ill-advised driving miscue we quickly realised that pro wrestling was as unrealistic as a Big Foot or Dead Elvis sighting and certainly much faker than the WrestleMania X toupee worn by the former Finkus Maximus.

photo: wrealano@aol.com

For generations a good old-fashioned wrestling feud would end in one of two ways, with either the glorious face (the good guy) wallowing in the glow and admiration of fans, overcoming the odds and posing with their newly-crowned hardware or with the dastardly heel (the bad guy) cheating and lying his way to the top and basking in the demise of the fallen hero. Regardless of the obvious outcomes to the world's most entertaining male soap opera, chances are the highly-contested feuds are culminated in some sort of over-the-top gimmick match:

THE GOOD, THE BAD AND THE KENNEL FROM HELL MATCH

THE GOOD

IRON MAN MATCH:

Usually set for 30 or 60 minutes, the wrestler with the most victories after that time is declared the winner. The most famous Iron Man Match was held at WrestleMania XII on March 31, 1996, when Shawn Michaels battled Bret Hart for the WWE title. After neither man scored a win during the first 60 minutes, Gorilla Monsoon, acting authority figure at the time, ordered the match to go into sudden death and well, the rest is sweet chin music history.

HELL IN A CELL:

Established in October 1997, this demonic structure has been the make or break for several wrestling stars over the years. The climax for most WWE feuds in recent memory, it has even garnered its very own pay-per-view event. Rikishi hayrides aside, perhaps one of the most brutal and iconic spectacles in the last two decades was that of Mankind being launched on to the Spanish announcers' booth by the Undertaker from the top of the Hell in a Cell cage in the summer of 1998. Sure his ear was torn off in Germany many years beforehand, but it was this match that forever solidified Mick Foley's status as the King of Hardcore.

LOSER LEAVES TOWN MATCH:

Not to be mistaken for the one-hit wonder 'Pink Slip on a Pole Match' during the late 90s Attitude era, this match is usually set up for wrestlers on

their way out and thus the 'storyline' ending is an orchestrated work to write the departed wrestler out of the company.

THE STEEL CAGE MATCH:

These days the steel cage is a watered-down gimmick match but during the 70s and 80s the cage was seen as a quintessential game changer. Just ask Don Muraco, Jimmy Snuka or even Paul Orndorff, whose *Saturday Night's Main Event* tie was the closest he ever came to WWF gold. Sorry Mr Wonderful, close only counts in horseshoes and hand grenades, not cage matches and immortal leg drops.

ROYAL RUMBLE MATCH:

First won by 'Hacksaw' Jim Duggan back in 1988, the Rumble match has become a wrestling institution and precursor to WrestleMania season. Raising the bar of the traditional battle royal concept, this match is a yearly tradition much like the Easter bunny, Santa Claus and the Survivor Series.

HOLLYWOOD BACKLOT BRAWL:

This once-in-a-lifetime match, which stole the WrestleMania show, came complete with a golden Cadillac, an OJ-inspired white bronco chase, a grown man in lingerie, and yes, a victory by the often imitated but never duplicated 'Rowdy' Roddy Piper.

THE BAD

BURIED ALIVE MATCH:

Chances are your feud with the Undertaker will end in one of three ways: a tombstone piledriver, a WrestleMania defeat or a notch in the loss column courtesy of the ill-fated Buried Alive Match. Several painfully wretched alternatives to this match exist in the form of the Casket Match (in order to win you must force your opponent into the ringside casket) and the Last Ride Match (same concept except the coffin is replaced by a hearse). These matches, although unique in their own right, are about as predictable as a chorus of boos during a Nikolai Volkoff Russian national anthem circa 1986.

KISS MY ASS MATCH:

Not to be confused with the Kiss My Ass Club; however, this painful gimmick match, which saw The Rock beat 'Mr Ass' Billy Gunn was far worse than Vince McMahon dropping his trousers on *Raw*, but perhaps not worse than Rocky Maivia's hair-raising Survivor Series debut or Kip James' Rockabilly misstep.

BLINDFOLD MATCH:

Much like the pink elephant in the room, this match between Jake 'The Snake' Roberts and Rick Martel sticks out like a sore thumb among the annals of pro wrestling gimmick matches. Aside from the most welcomed DDT in WrestleMania history, this match helped usher the 'boring' chant into the national pay-per-view spotlight.

WORLD WAR 3 MATCH:

Three rings, 60 wrestlers and four pay-per-views later, World War 3 never made quite the impact that Turner brass had hoped. The inaugural event, won by 'Macho Man' Randy Savage, featured a collection of the best and worst of WCW's power plant (Sgt. Craig Pittman and Sgt. Buddy Lee Parker) not to mention the likes of VK Wallstreet, Big Train Bart, Max Muscle and 'Pistol' Pez Whatley.

SCAFFOLD MATCH:

Snacking on danger and dining on death is one thing but partaking in the ill-fated scaffold match at Starrcade '86 is maybe not such a great idea. Fortunately for the Road Warriors and Midnight Express, the only injury in this one-dimensional match was when Jim Cornette fell off and busted his knee during a post-match squabble.

EMPTY ARENA MATCH:

If Janet Jackson exposing a nipple slip during Super Bowl half-time was a mistake then WWE's Halftime Heat between The Rock and Mankind was a very close second. Speaking of close second, this list cannot be complete without mention of WCW's King of the Road Match between Dustin Rhodes and the Blacktop Bully.

From the creators of the Mae

THE KENNEL
FROM HELL

Young hand birth and the Brawl for All series, this combination of steel cages and canines brought new meaning to the term lame. As Al Snow and Big Boss Man fought over the prestigious hardcore title, the true essence of this once epic battle was summed up literally by the dog crap left surrounding the ring.

10 SIDESLAMMERS

TEN DREAM MATCHES WE'D PAY TO SEE

1. Hulk Hogan vs. Ric Flair in the 1980s
2. Stone Cold Steve Austin vs. Macho Man Randy Savage
3. The Rock vs. Andre the Giant
4. Stone Cold vs. Hulk Hogan
5. Sting vs. Undertaker
6. Ric Flair from the 1970s vs. Ric Flair (present day)
7. Santino Marella vs. George the Animal Steele
8. Vince McMahon vs. Ted Turner (at height of Monday Night Wars)
9. The Road Warriors vs. The Dudleys
10. Jimmy Snuka vs. Ricky Steamboat vs. Rey Mysterio

Before the days of general managers and special guest hosts the 'storyline' authority figure belonged to one man, and that man was the distinguished Jack Tunney. In the summer of 1984 Tunney was brought in as the federation's figurehead president, and he was used to make major storyline announcements, suspensions and title changes, as well as create plenty of riveting and controversial decisions that would further ongoing feuds. Among his many memorable appearances and 'decisions', Tunney was a huge part of most, if not all, of the company's major headlines during the golden age of Hulkamania.

He once suspended rogue referee Danny Davis 'for life' due to his awful officiating and his favouritism towards the heel wrestlers such as the Hart Foundation, who captured the tag titles due to Davis not calling it right down the middle. He also stripped 'Million Dollar Man' Ted DiBiase of the WWF title after he successfully purchased the belt from Andre the Giant. This decision alone led to the now famous 14-man title tournament won by 'Macho Man' Randy Savage at WrestleMania IV. Among other things, he suspended the Islanders for kidnapping the British Bulldogs' mascot Matilda and even had Ric Flair's 'real' world title distorted during television promos leading up to his big showdown with Hulk Hogan. Tunney was a major on-air figure during arguably the World Wrestling Federation's most popular era. However, being forced out of the company in the fall of 1995, the Tunney presidency had eventually run its course and the on-air role of WWF leadership was handed to Gorilla Monsoon. Tunney's legacy, however, will always be remembered as both well-respected and less combative than most on-air leadership roles of today. In all honesty, how many superstars can lay claim to 'banning' snakes at ringside and more impressively placing a 'gag order' on Jesse 'The Body' Ventura? That distinction, my friends, belongs solely to 'President' Jack Tunney.

MR FAKE PRESIDENT

photo:Wrealano@aol.com

AKEEM IS ONE MAN GANG

AND OTHER REBRANDINGS THAT INSULTED OUR INTELLIGENCE

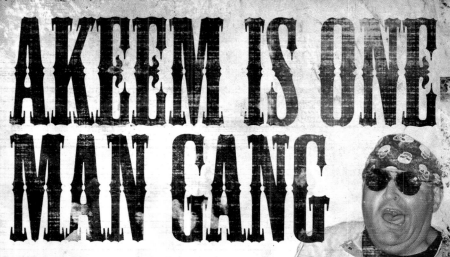

Beyonce once said if you like it you should put a ring on it. Well, wrestling companies often say if you don't like it, they'll put a mask on it or change it altogether. Yes, when one superstar fails to 'get over' or is becoming stale, he'll be repackaged in some way. Sometimes it's intentionally transparent and successful like when Bradshaw ditched the APA gimmick in favour of the cowboy hat wearing, money-basking heel John Bradshaw Layfield – but other instances are less successful. Fans can totally understand when a wrestler needs to be repackaged with a new gimmick like Bradshaw or, to name drop another two: Tugboat as Typhoon or Rick Martel turning into 'The Model', but changing a wrestler's identity altogether is lame. Yet, for years, wrestling higher-ups tried to pull the wool over our eyes.

It was clear to every wrestling fan and even 'Mean' Gene Okerlund that when Akeem debuted on television with Slick by his side, he wasn't a new talent from 'The Lion King' continent. Nope. He was the recovered One Man Gang. Gang had been a top heel at one time, but

Boss Man as the tag team 'The Twin Towers'. It didn't stop with that African nightmare. There have been countless examples of this happening like when Brutus Beefcake became Hulk Hogan's 'Disciple' in WCW. On the flipside, the move does sometimes work. Despite WWE not acknowledging that he was indeed one half of the tandem 3-Minute Warning, Umaga became a strong heel for the company in 2006. Joined by obnoxious manager Armando Alejandro Estrada, Umaga squashed his opponents each week with his signature thumb to the throat, and even went on to headline WrestleMania XXIII in the infamous 'Trump shaving McMahon' gimmick match. But, come on… we knew Edward Fatu, who had been wrestling as Jamal, was Umaga. Throwing Samoan tattoos on his face and changing his attire didn't exactly make us forget who he once was. On an unrelated note, did you know 'Leaping' Lanny Poffo was 'The Genius?'

when he took the character as far as he could go, he was rebranded an 'African Dream'. You can throw a medallion around his neck and a kufi on his head, but no respectable wrestling fan would've believed that he was a fresh face in the WWF.

The WWF played fans as saps and ran with the gimmick – giving Akeem a huge push with the Big

SIDESLAMMERS

UNFORGETTABLE GIMMICK MAKEOVERS

Steve Keirn – The Skinner
Barry Windham – The Stalker
Johnny Polo – Raven
Tony Atlas – Saba Simba
Demolition Smash – Repo Man

Oz – Vinnie Vegas – Diesel
Papa Shango – Kama Mustafa – The Godfather
Iron Sheik – Col. Mustafa
Isaac Yankem – Kane
Sparky Plugg – Hardcore Holly

VIDEO KILLED THE WRESTLING STAR?

WWE continues to release collections of their superstars' entrance music and tracks inspired by their in-ring heroes, but one thing that hasn't happened since – roughly – the release of the 'Land of Confusion' Ronald Reagan puppet, is an accompanying music video featuring wrestling talent. We can speculate why this sadly doesn't happen anymore. For starters, every music video the then WWF put out back in the day painfully reflected the decade they were made in – the 1980s. Whether it was terrible fashions or 'cutting edge' graphics that looked as if they were created on a Lite Brite, each video plays like a bad one-night stand. In other words, it's probably something the company will eternally regret. But, they shouldn't.

We long for the days of wrestlers trying to look cool and tough as they sang off key and danced with two left boots. Who could forget the music videos for 'Land of a Thousand Dances' and 'If You Only Knew'? Well, no one

photo:Wrealano@aol.com

thanks to YouTube. The first video has its moments – like the mere pleasure in knowing Uncle Elmer probably appeared on MTV at one point – but the latter is just heinous. The song is bad, and the video is delightfully worse. The music video is essentially a montage of wrestling highlights packaged with footage of talent reciting their lines – almost rapping – in front of a neon backdrop. The best the video has to offer is a 'We Are The World' ending with all the talent reciting the nails-on-a-chalkboard chorus. It's funny now, but if

photo:Wrestland.com

to Frankie's caretaker for crooning on the aforementioned 'If You Only Knew' video.

In the years prior to and after 'Piledriver', other music videos were made, but none of them appeared worthy of *Dial MTV*. Take Robbie Dupree's instant classic 'Girls In Cars' for example, which served as the theme song for the Tito Santana/Rick Martel tandem Strike Force. Rocking out with his guitar and mom jeans on the beach – Dupree was no relation to Rene, by the way – this video should've been a one-hit wonder. It's quite a scene watching the bearded singer rock out in a music video so complex that it can only be described as a video with… wait for it… girls in cars. Oh, and there were seagulls, too.

There were many other notable videos – like Slick's 'Jive Soul Bro', which we're guessing set African American people back a decade or two (fried chicken + pimp suits = um, racism?) – but arguably the best music video of all time to feature wrestlers had little to do with any storyline or album.

Cyndi Lauper's 'Goonies R Good Enough' music video is the holy grail of grappling music videos. With a host of cameos including Roddy Piper, the Fabulous Moolah, the Iron Sheik, and Lauper regular Capt. Lou Albano, the video to the mega-hit 'The Goonies' has it all: great music, incomprehensible storylines, and even Nikolai Volkoff milking a plastic cow. If this music video still doesn't make you want to do the Truffle shuffle – nothing will!

I was a WWE studio head, I would've cut the entire music video budget altogether by the time Bill Clinton reached office.

Another nostalgic music video trip from the WWF is the 'Piledriver' video, in which the wrestlers double as construction workers. Yes, even 'Superstar' Billy Graham was up for a day of drilling after his meatball surgery! It's pretty comical to watch now, but one can appreciate Koko B. Ware singing his parts like Mariah Carey while wearing a hard hat, and using a sledgehammer like a musical instrument. On a related note, props

5 SIDESLAMMERS

FIVE OTHER STARS WHO WOULD'VE FIT WELL IN THE GOONIES VIDEO

1. Jimmy Snuka
2. Randy Savage
3. Goldust
4. Santino Marella
5. The APA

WHO BETTA THAN KANYON?

The WWE/WCW Invasion angle of 2001 could've been handled differently, and executed a lot better. Wow... talk about understatements. At the very least, they could've made WCW legend Ric Flair or the nWo integral parts of the invasion but the WWE higher-ups couldn't wait for them to get their respective affairs in order and jumped the gun on the angle.

Instead of a groundbreaking storyline of a defunct wrestling company waging war on their former chief competitor, the Invasion angle and subsequent WCW/ECW 'Alliance' saw – for the most part – B-list stars taking on A-list WWE superstars. With the exception of Booker T, Rob Van Dam, and arguably Stacey Keibler, the big angle was a big bust. That said, there was one star shining above the

shaky storyline and it wasn't one half of Harlem Heat or the artist formerly known as Miss Hancock.

As he had done in WCW numerous times, Chris Kanyon delivered for WWE but we'll get to that in a minute. Unfortunately, throughout his career, quality storylines were hard for the talented grappler to come by. So were respectable pushes. But, Kanyon did the best with what he was given and always rose above it. When he started out, he jobbed. When his tag team Men at Work (construction worker wrestlers – really?) didn't, well, work, he was reborn as the masked Mortis. When the entertaining but one-dimensional Mortis' time was up, he ditched the mask and feuded with Raven.

Following the feud and ultimate partnership with the head of The

Flock, Kanyon joined Diamond Dallas Page (DDP) and Bam Bam Bigelow as part of the 'Jersey Triad' stable. While that group showed promise and even resulted in some gold, it ultimately dissolved quicker than a post-*Clerks* Kevin Smith movie.

By 1999, Kanyon was repackaged again as Chris 'Champagne' Kanyon, a man with a deep appreciation of the good life. That bubbly gimmick fizzled, but a storyline involving DDP set his career off. After being thrown off a triple cage by Mike Awesome, who had his share of bad gimmicks by the way, Kanyon turned his attention against DDP and a feud and hilarious heel turn was born.

Making fun of Page any chance he could get, Kanyon reinvented himself as 'Positively' Kanyon – a knock on DDP's autobiography *Positively Page*. During his story arc with the Diamond Cutter – which happened during WCW's short-lived 'New Blood' storyline – he donned an over-the-top blond wig, exploited DDP's catchphrase of 'feel the bang', and even stole his opponent's finisher. Among the many highlights the wrestler had during this period was giving beloved 'Mean' Gene Okerlund a 'Kanyon Kutter'.

Up until the end of WCW, Kanyon primarily battled the 'self-high five' star. When he finally arrived in WWE, however, he was thrown into a DDP-less arena. During the forgettable Invasion, he teamed with fellow 'Alliance' members Shawn Stasiak and Hugh Morrus and defeated the Big Show, Albert and Billy Gunn. Shortly thereafter, he was given the WCW United States Championship by Booker T, but eventually lost it to Tajiri. He'd also be rebranded as 'The Alliance MVP', a name that never really stuck but launched a hilarious rhetorical question which audience members ate up: 'Who betta than Kanyon?'

Kanyon could've been bigger in WWE, but injuries kept him out of action and pushes never came to fruition when he was healthy. Some highlights, however, included winning the then-WWF Tag Team belts with long-time nemesis DDP and impersonating Boy George during a battle between the Big Show and the Undertaker. Yes, you read that right.

On April 2, 2010, Kanyon, who had suffered from bipolar disorder, was found dead of an apparent suicide. Wrestling fans will miss his unique wrestling style and wonderful sense of humour. Who betta than Kanyon? Not many.

10 SIDESLAMMERS

TEN OPPONENTS THE UNDERTAKER WILL NEVER FACE AT WRESTLEMANIA

1. Festus
2. D'Lo Brown
3. Marty Jannetty
4. Tank Abbott
5. Alex Wright
6. Disco Inferno
7. Dean Malenko
8. Hornswoggle
9. Hillbilly Jim
10. Billy Ocean

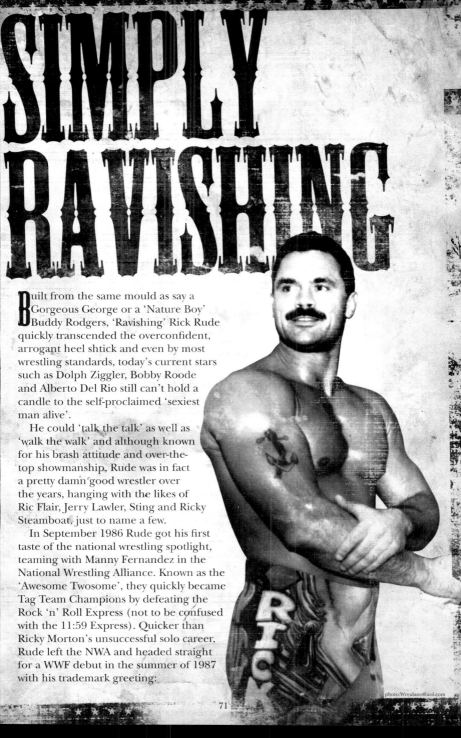

SIMPLY RAVISHING

Built from the same mould as say a Gorgeous George or a 'Nature Boy' Buddy Rodgers, 'Ravishing' Rick Rude quickly transcended the overconfident, arrogant heel shtick and even by most wrestling standards, today's current stars such as Dolph Ziggler, Bobby Roode and Alberto Del Rio still can't hold a candle to the self-proclaimed 'sexiest man alive'.

He could 'talk the talk' as well as 'walk the walk' and although known for his brash attitude and over-the-top showmanship, Rude was in fact a pretty damn good wrestler over the years, hanging with the likes of Ric Flair, Jerry Lawler, Sting and Ricky Steamboat, just to name a few.

In September 1986 Rude got his first taste of the national wrestling spotlight, teaming with Manny Fernandez in the National Wrestling Alliance. Known as the 'Awesome Twosome', they quickly became Tag Team Champions by defeating the Rock 'n' Roll Express (not to be confused with the 11:59 Express). Quicker than Ricky Morton's unsuccessful solo career, Rude left the NWA and headed straight for a WWF debut in the summer of 1987 with his trademark greeting:

photo:Wrealano@aol.com

What I'd like to have right now is for all you (insert city and insult) keep the noise down while I take my robe off and show the ladies what a real man is supposed to look like.

With his signature ring entrance and superb mic skills, Rude's star was on the rise. His first major feud was with Jake 'The Snake' Roberts, which was centred around his wife Cheryl, who was reluctantly chosen at ringside by Rude's manager Bobby 'The Brain' Heenan to kiss the chiselled grappler after one of his many Saturday morning jabroni beat-downs. His most famous federation feud was with the Ultimate Warrior (formerly Dingo, currently insane) that began in 1989 at the Royal Rumble 'Super Posedown'. Thanks to a metal pose bar, Rude got the best of the Warrior to conclude the posedown and, thanks to Heenan, the 'Ravishing One' captured the Intercontinental title from the Parts Unknown native at that year's WrestleMania.

In October 1991, Rude headed back to NWA/WCW, revealing himself to be the Halloween Phantom at the Halloween Havoc pay-per-view. The most anti-climactic masked wrestler since Dusty Rhodes' Midnight Rider, Rude later helped lead the Dangerous Alliance against the company's top faces. With help from Paul E. Dangerously, Arn Anderson and 'Stunning' Steve Austin, the heel super group was a collection of bad guys reminiscent of the days of the *Challenge of the Super Friends* animated series that featured 13 recurring villains known as the Legion of Doom.

In 1994, during a match against Sting in Japan, Rude suffered a career-threatening injury that quickly forced him into early retirement. Two years later and after a brief stint as an ECW colour commentator, Rude returned to the WWF as the 'insurance policy' of the pre-watered-down version of D-Generation X. However on November 17, 1997, Rick Rude made wrestling history by appearing on WWF *Raw* and WCW *Monday Nitro* on the same evening. Performing with WWF on a 'pay-per-appearance' contract, Rude appeared on a live *Nitro* in full mustache glory tearing Shawn Michaels a new one as well as referring to the WWF as the Titanic (an obvious reference to a sinking ship and not the sappy Celine Dion movie soundtrack). One hour later or six days earlier (*Raw* was pre-taped every other week) Rude stood alongside his fellow DX brethren in all his full bad guy beard glory. Rude spent the next year or so as a member of the New World Order.

In 1999, while rumoured to be training for a comeback to active wrestling, Rick Rude passed away at the age of 40. His unmistakable charisma and arrogant flair made him one of the top wrestlers in the business and there is no doubt that he was and always will be 'Simply Ravishing'.

THE WIZARD OF ODD

a meatball parm hero, Graham was an innovative and charismatic superstar that paved the way for the likes of both Jesse 'The Body' Ventura and 'Hollywood' Hulk Hogan. The Wizard and Graham clearly set the bar for the Austins and the Ortons of the world, who despite being labelled as anti-

Originally introduced as Abdullah Farouk, manager of the fireball-tossing Original Sheik, Ernie Roth was soon introduced to WWF audiences as the Grand Wizard of Wrestling. Sporting his trademark sunglasses, flamboyant suit jacket and over-the-top turban, the Grand Wizard soon became the measuring stick for what the heel manager aspired to be. On December 1, 1973, the Wizard managed Stan 'The Man' Stasiak to a WWF Championship victory over Pedro Morales. There's no telling what effect the Grand Wizard would have had on the career of the former world champion's son Shawn, who is remembered mostly for his wrestling gimmick, Meat. But enough of 'Planet Stasiak' and let us focus on the managerial genius of Roth and his much-hated Wizard persona.

On April 30, 1977, the heel manager helped guide 'Superstar' Billy Graham to the WWF Title in a shocking upset over 'The Living Legend' Bruno Sammartino. Before his televised hip surgery during his mid-80s comeback that may or may not have closely resembled

photo:Wrealano@aol.com

heroes, were cheered and helped sell out arenas night after night despite their dastardly ways.

Among his other accolades, the Wizard also managed the very first Intercontinental Champion Pat Patterson as well as some of wrestling's top villains throughout the decade of disco including Ken Patera, 'The Magnificent' Don Muraco, Ox Baker, The Masked Superstar, Ernie Ladd and 'The Russian Bear' Ivan Koloff. Despite his untimely death in 1983, the Grand Wizard was a managerial pioneer posthumously inducted into the WWE Hall of Fame in 1995 and forever known for making life miserable for baby-face wrestlers across the world.

HOLD ON TO DUSTY'S JEWELS

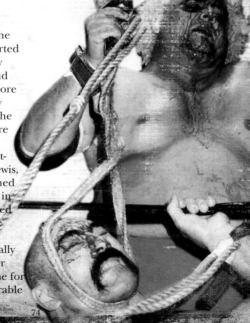

Some mysteries in wrestling are better left unsolved, such as why was Mike Tyson, well known as the 'Baddest Man on the Planet', escorted to the ring at WrestleMania XIV by corporate stooges Pat Patterson and Gerald Brisco? Or perhaps even more mysterious was the introduction by 'Precious' Paul Ellering of Rocco the ventriloquist dummy used to inspire the legendary Road Warriors.

Then of course there is the short-lived wrestling career of Juanita Lewis, the portly but enthusiastic fan turned manager known as Sapphire. Clad in their matching black outfits adorned with hideous yellow polka dots, the former Princess Dark Cloud was partnered with the iconic and equally flamboyant Dusty Rhodes. However short in stature, Lewis made a name for herself during her brief yet memorable stint by teaming up with the son of a plumber at WrestleMania VI against 'Macho King' Randy Savage and 'Sensational Queen' Sherri

Before exiting the federation, 'Sweet' Sapphire proved once and for all that 'everybody's got a price for the Million Dollar Man'. Sadly, as much as we want to remember Sapphire for her polka-dot toting dance moves with Goldust's

dad, it will be the lasting impression of the reluctant Lewis ironing Ted DiBiase's money that is etched in our wrestling subconscious forever.

Oh, who are we kidding? Her wrestling shelf life may have been cut short but if Dusty was the 'American Dream' then by all means Sapphire lived the 'American Wet Dream'.

THE SNUG-SHIRTED CHEAP POP

In the world of professional wrestling, valets are usually big on looks while managers are usually big on personality. In the late 1990s, however, WCW broke the mould and went with neither to escort rising star Chris Jericho to the ring. The following is a story about how one slob made it in the land of Nitro Girls and the nWo.

John Riker was supposedly a truck driver for the now defunct Ted Turner company when he was 'hired' by Jericho to be his personal security guard. Under the name Ralphus, Riker walked Jericho to the ring with a snug half-shirt exposing the best beer gut in wrestling history. While Jericho displayed his signature grand mic skills, Ralphus was motionless and expressionless but seemed somewhat fun-loving. His stint in the WCW didn't last long, and his contributions to the business were smaller than the stained snug shirts he used to wear, but he was a memorable outside-the-box

experiment that paid off in giggles. While Ralphus is synonymous with the early days of the Lion Tamer, he actually outlived Jericho in the Atlanta company. When Jericho left for WWF, Riker was paired with Norman Smiley for a brief time. That odd pairing, however, didn't pay off, and Ralphus and his beer gut have been missing in action ever since. Hopefully, he's trucking on somewhere in a baby doll tee.

He wasn't the biggest, baddest, or best ever, but when it came to taking bumps, there was arguably no one better than Crash Holly. An underrated innovator who had so much more personality than his fake cousin Hardcore Holly, this Anaheim native revolutionised hardcore wrestling in the WWF/WWE with his wrestling prowess and hardcore gimmick.

Holly, who had wrestled for independents under various names (The Leprechaun!) and briefly in ECW before landing in the WWF/WWE, won the Hardcore Championship a record 22 times in McMahon Land, and had some wonderful television moments thanks to his concept of defending the title any time, any place, and anywhere; 24 hours a day, seven days a week – so long as a ref was there. Dubbed the 'Houdini of Hardcore', Holly always seemed to steal his fair share of victories by hitting unsuspecting hardcore champs with something to regain a championship he had probably just lost in a similar manner.

(Opponents would often take advantage of the '24/7' rule by jumping Holly anywhere from a Laundromat to a circus and he responded in similar situations.)

In addition to his hardcore legacy, Holly, who died of an apparent suicide on November 6, 2003 – just four months after joining TNA following his WWE release – leaves behind years of humorous highlights and several key wrestling accomplishments. Focusing on the former, we'll never forget how he hilariously claimed to weigh 400 pounds in order to compete as a heavyweight. Looking at the latter, he won numerous championships without the use of a chair shot. Some notable victories included he and tag team partner Hardcore Holly defeating The Rock 'n' Sock Connection for the WWF Tag Team titles, and winning the European Championship and Light Heavyweight Championship.

While he doesn't get as many headlines as other dearly departed superstars, we remember Crash Holly as a complete original in an industry with its share of often duplicated jabronis.

THE GREAT ESCAPE ARTIST

As wrestling superstars such as John Cena and The Rock have begun reaching out to fans through various social networking sites such as Twitter and Facebook, it is hard to imagine what the wrestling world, or more importantly, how the career of Zack Ryder, would have turned out without the help of these various outlets. But seriously, who are we kidding, right?

American street cred by body-slamming the close-to-600-pound Yokozuna on the dock of New York City's USS *Intrepid*, and who knows, it was probably the most patriotic event to happen in the WWF since Corporal Kirchner's first promo.

Following the 'All-American' slam was the 'Lex Express' campaign tour. Travelling all across the United States

ALL ABOARD THE LEX EXPRESS

As the 'King of the Broskis' tried to petition his way up the championship ladder in WWE we can only imagine the impact Twitter would have had on the campaign trail that Lex Luger began way back when in the summer of 1993.

In essence Luger was up at the plate with two strikes against him. As a spokesman for the McMahon-influenced World Bodybuilding Federation, (which lasted just as long as the XFL) as well as 'The Narcissist' gimmick complete with 'Total Package' posedowns in front of several full-length mirrors before each match, it was clear that Luger's time in the WWF was going nowhere fast.

It wasn't until July 4, 1993, that Lex Luger, thanks in part to the departure of the Hulkster, earned instant in his red, white and blue bus, Luger greeted fans and petitioned for a title shot against the WWF Champion, Yokozuna. You can only imagine how much gas Luger would have saved if Twitter had been around in the early 90s.

Luger's only shot was a miss-fire at SummerSlam that year, resulting in a count-out victory over the champion. Between lengthy feuds with the likes of Ludvig Borga and Tatanka, the Lex Express never reached the same heights as that hot summer day on the *Intrepid* and just two years later the ride was officially over when Lex Luger shockingly jumped ship and appeared on the first ever episode of *Nitro*, helping Eric Bischoff and company fire the first of many shots in the now infamous Monday Night Wrestling Wars.

BROKEBACK WRESTLING

THE BALLAD OF BILLY AND CHUCK

The WWE has had its share of flamboyantly-fuelled tag teams over the years. Take for example The Dicks and The Heavenly Bodies, not to mention in more recent years The Heartthrobs. No team, however, captured more success than the partnership between Billy Gunn and Chuck Palumbo collectively known simply as Billy and Chuck.

During a time when tag team wrestling was at a premium led by the

photo:Wrealano@aol.com

Hardy Boys, the APA and the Dudley Boyz *sans* Dances With Dudley of course, Billy and Chuck managed to capture not one but two WWE World Tag Team Championships.

Led by their personal stylist Rico and accentuated by their matching red ring trunks, bath robes and bleached blond hair, the affectionate duo even won the prestigious PWI Tag Team of the Year award in 2002. Despite a successful singles run as well as several tag team stints as a member of the Smoking Gunns and New Age Outlaws, the former Mr Ass finally found mainstream success by teaming with the one-time member of the Full Blooded Italians. Much like George Skaaland was the pride of White Plains, Billy and Chuck were the pride of… well, let's just say they were the pride of good old-fashioned tag team wrestling in the early 2000s. In the autumn of 2002 Chuck proposed to Billy but during the publicly-televised commitment ceremony on *Smackdown*, it was the 'Ass Man' that got cold feet. Meanwhile the truth was revealed that the very-up-close-and-personal-beyond-tag-team-partnership between Billy and Chuck was just a publicity stunt.

10 SIDE ★ SLAMMERS

TEN NOT-SO-DYNAMIC DUOS
1. Power & Glory
2. Rhythm and Blues
3. The Basham Brothers
4. Heidenreich and Animal
5. Jumping Bomb Angels
6. High Energy
7. Dick Butkis and Vince 'XFL' McMahon
8. The 11:59 Express
9. The Mulkeys
10. Three-Minute Warning

ADRIAN ADONIS:

MORE THAN JUST FLOWER POWER

When he debuted in the mid-1970s, Keith Franke AKA Adrian Adonis quickly made a name for himself in the American Wrestling Association (AWA) with his skilled (and swift) ring approach, tough-guy swagger and signature leather jacket. As we know, by the mid-1980s, Adonis would reach the pinnacle of his career by going from leather to lace and undergoing the most bewildering gimmick change in WWF/WWE and wrestling history. Yes, there are heel turns, and then their high heel turns. But, before we talk about 'Adorable' Adrian Adonis, let's paint a picture of the man before he literally smelled the roses.

As we were saying, Adonis took off alongside Jesse (pre-'The Body') Ventura in the AWA as the East-West Connection, earning credibility as a dominant tag team – so much so that the pair was lured to the World Wrestling Federation together. When Ventura was out of the picture, Adonis shined as a singles competitor and eventually tagged with a real Dick... Texan Dick Murdoch. While the pair won the tag team titles together, Adonis seemed poised as a solo heel but needed a twist. In other words, the dreadful biker's hat and belt around his neck wasn't cutting it anymore. After a failed run with managing royalty

Bobby 'The Brain' Heenan, Adonis, who regularly cut promos on how unappreciated he was, aligned himself with Jimmy Hart and soon let his freak flag fly and by that, we don't mean he entered the ring to a bad Hart song ('Eat Your Heart Out Rick Springfield' probably didn't go platinum).

Following stints in which he carried a briefcase handcuffed to his wrist and brought perfume – appropriately called 'Fragrance' – to the ring, he shed his leather jacket (which he gave to Roddy Piper on another classic 'Piper's Pit'), and became 'Adorable' Adrian Adonis. Yes, before there was Billy or Chuck, there was AAA – a man with bleached blond hair, who wore pink outfits that Punky Brewster wouldn't be caught dead in, and more eye shadow than a hooker on the Freemont end of Vegas at 3:30 a.m. But thanks to his agility and strong mic skills, the big man in blush was a top heel in the WWF for a couple of years, scoring matches at WrestleManias II and III, and feuds with everyone from Junkyard Dog to Hulk Hogan.

While he lost a title match to the Hulkster, his popularity only grew thanks to 'The Flower Shop', Adonis' 'show' that temporarily replaced the Pit. The show featured many memorable 'episodes', but arguably

the best ones were when Piper arrived back and the pair battled each other on their respective sets. After weeks and weeks of feuding (and Cowboy Bob Orton donning a pink cowboy hat), the two met in an epic 'Hair vs. Hair' match at WrestleMania III. Piper would win, and Brutus 'The Barber' Beefcake would go on to shave Adonis bald. Surprisingly, a feud between Beefcake and Adonis was short-lived when Adonis left WWF for the AWA. By 1988, he was slated to compete in New Japan Pro Wrestling (he was a respected and non-flamboyant star over there), but got injured and could not travel overseas. On July 4 of that year, in one of the most bizarre deaths in wrestling history, Adonis was killed along with two other wrestlers when driver (and fellow wrestler Mike Kelly) swerved off a road in Newfoundland to avoid hitting a moose, and fell into a lake instead. As sad as it was, it's fitting that Adonis, just 33 when he died, had a bizarre death, because his career was so delightfully bizarre.

In 1987, while the sea of yellow and red was running wild all over the wrestling world and selling out arenas across the States night after night, perhaps the hardest-working guy on the card was a relative unknown by the name of Dan Marsh. Of course, to wrestling fans Marsh is better known as former referee turned wrestler 'Dangerous' Danny Davis, who not only worked in favour of the WWF's top villains but unbeknown to many casual wrestling fans he occasionally donned a wrestling mask and appeared as perennial masked jobber, Mr X.

Despite his double duty, the late

THE
CROOKED
REF

80s the Parts Unknown, Rhode Island native revolutionised the ref business by becoming a bigger story than the actual grapplers themselves, which culminated in a WrestleMania III victory along with the Hart Foundation against Tito Santana and the British Bulldogs. No doubt the crowd reaction to the Davis debacle helped put the wheels in motion for the double Hebner fiasco that occurred just less than one year later on a primetime episode of *Saturday Night's Main Event*. Despite several recent miscues and referee backstabs, most notably Nick Patrick's nWo favouritism and the Sylvan Granier screwjob that almost single-handedly sabotaged the long-awaited Hulk Hogan vs. Vince McMahon feud, 'Dangerous' Danny Davis is the cream of the crop when it comes to bad officiating.

FOWL PLAY: WRESTLING LAYS AN EGG

Professional wrestling has laid its fair share of eggs over the years but literally none more rotten than the one laid on November 22, 1990. Hatched before our very eyes at the Survivor Series after weeks of speculation, the shroud of Thanksgiving mystery was finally hatched in front of a sold-out crowd at the Hartford Civic Center. Much like the Shockmaster falling flat on his face or having to sit through a match featuring the Dungeon of Doom's Loch Ness, the Gobbledy Gooker's in-ring debut segment was well on its way to being a disaster with or without 'Mean' Gene Okerlund's botched cartwheel. Dressed in a feathered suit with all the trimmings, veteran wrestler Hector Guerrero's turkey run in WWE lasted as long as a 42-inch HDTV at Target on Black Friday.

Ever since the boo-birds expressed their heartfelt gratitude over 20 years ago, the Gooker has since made a few rare appearances in the WWE. At 2001's WrestleMania X-Seven the world's most famous wrestling bird not named Koko or Frankie returned to his pay-per-view roots and took part in the Gimmick Battle Royal. Seven years later at the Survivor Series the Boogeyman borrowed Guerrero's old digs and terrified Carlito and Primo. On November 23, 2009, a day and 19 years since pop culture's second-most embarrassing hatching (go ahead, Google Mork and Mindy's son Mearth, we dare you) the Gooker was unmasked to be former diva Maryse who had dressed up as the wrestling fowl in order to sneak-attack her arch-rival Melina.

Ironically on the same debut night that Hector Guerrero donned the turkey feathers and shat the biggest wrestling load this side of 'Nasty' Ned Brady, a relative unknown named Mark Calaway was giving wrestling fans a taste of his Deadman persona for the very first time.

THE LEGEND OF JIMMY JACK FUNK

How disappointed were you when you found out Hulk Hogan and Brutus Beefcake were not really brothers? Sure, maybe not as anti-climactic as learning that Paul Orndorff rose from the dead only to own a bowling alley in the suburbs of Atlanta, Georgia.

But let's be truthfully honest – these days everyone is the Hulkster's 'brother' whether the big guy is sharing commercial airtime with Troy Aikman or even baring it all on the *Howard Stern Show*. That being said, 'wrestling brothers' has become a thing of the past and its final resting place remains on the shelf between the likes of Nidia and Tekno Team 2000.

Among the most celebrated 'brothers' in professional wrestling were also some of the greatest tag teams the world has ever seen. For those of you with the benefits of flash photography, Edge and Christian were born, bred and hailed from Toronto, Canada but although they were billed as 'brothers' during the Brood era they were just really close friends. Just as convincing as Justin Bieber pawning off his own cologne was the fact that Bubba Ray and Devon Dudley came from the same womb. Even a former dentist turned Fake Diesel was given a mask and we were left to believe that

photo:Wrealano@aol.com

the 'Big Red Monster', Kane, was in fact the Undertaker's brother.

The most infamous of all wrestling-related 'brothers', however, was the long-lost sibling of the legendary Terry and Dory Funk. In 1986 the pre-pubescent universe of the WWE was introduced to Jimmy Jack Funk, clad in mask and traditional Funk cowboy boots. Managed by Jimmy Hart, the forgotten member of the Funk clan was actually played by veteran wrestler Jesse Barr, and to add fuel to the Funk fire, Barr was and is the only wrestler ever to wrestle with a noose around his neck.

With the exception of in-and-out-of-action legend Goldust or Sting, who continues to pay homage to cult actors in cult roles who died young (respectively Brandon Lee's Crow and Heath Ledger's Joker), make-up has become a lost art form in wrestling. Back in the 1980s and even the 1990s, you'd be hard pressed to find a time period when a wrestler donning make-up didn't exist and thrive in the wrestling world. Whether it was the

or blush (RIP Adrian Adonis) could lead to an instant cheap pop. We're guessing make-up isn't quite as big nowadays because the 1980s – the decade in which many stars hid behind painted faces – was more glam than today's world. It's either that or the fact the Boogeyman or Rico ruined make-up for wrestlers forever.

WHEN MAKE-UP WASN'T ONLY FOR DIVAS

Ultimate Warrior, Kamala, the Road Warriors or their clones Demolition, if you wanted to stand out in the business, you had to sport some impressive fake face tattoos.

Nowadays, wrestling talent will put on a mask or sport a unique facial trait (we're talking to you Santino 'uni-brow' Marella) to either add some mystery or expand on their character, but we long for the days when putting on a little face paint

ONE WARRIOR NATION

Almost as blatantly rude as Pippa Middleton's rear end trying to outshine the Royal Wedding was the WCW's decision to centre the much-anticipated Ultimate Warrior vs. Hulk Hogan re-match on the talentless exploits of the 'Disciple' Brutus Beefcake. Filed under 'wrestling train wreck' next to the ill-fated Tuxedo Match and the career of Tyson Tomko, One Warrior Nation completely missed the *Nitro* boat. Speaking of misses, it was Davey Boy Smith whose WCW run was cut short, no thanks to taking a bump on one of the Warrior's trap doors that was set up in the ring that landed the Bulldog in the hospital and sadly without a job. To make matters worse, when the WrestleMania VI main event re-match finally went down and the dust was clear, a victorious Hulkster only had one man to thank and that was his chair-wielding nephew Horace Hogan.

KURT ANGLE:

SHAVED HEAD LED TO FUNNY BONE LOSS

Kurt Angle is among the best athletes to ever perform in a wrestling ring. Oh, it's true. It's damn true. But, one thing that's been forgotten – especially since his last run in WWE and his current tenure in TNA – is just how funny the Olympic gold medallist once was. It's hard to believe given the former Team Angle leader's ferocious demeanour over the past five years or so, but Angle was once a humorous self-deprecating mic skills master.

Who could forget how many scenes he stole from 'Stone Cold' Steve Austin during the age of Invasion and the 'What?' era? You know, a time when Angle and Austin were vying for Vince McMahon's affections by either playing guitar for him or sporting matching cowboy hats (remember Angle's mini-hat?) We miss those days of him being a dopey, funny gold medallist out of the ring, contradicting his all-business in-ring persona beautifully. C'mon Kurt… just one more version of 'Jimmy Crack Corn and I don't care… I've got Olympic Gold' before retirement!

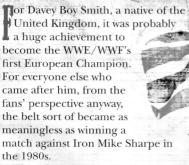

For Davey Boy Smith, a native of the United Kingdom, it was probably a huge achievement to become the WWE/WWF's first European Champion. For everyone else who came after him, from the fans' perspective anyway, the belt sort of became as meaningless as winning a match against Iron Mike Sharpe in the 1980s.

The title was created in the late 1990s and served as a springboard for some

POINTLESS GOLD AKA ALL OUT OF EUROS

rising stars to start their careers. Never carrying the international prestige that WWE/WWF suits probably hoped it would, the belt made more waves in the business for its long vacancies and ho-hum victories. Focusing on the former, who could forget when Shane McMahon decided to hide the belt in his bag for a few months in 1999? Yes, you read that right.

By July 22, 2002, the belt – which was won by everyone from D'Lo Brown to DDP – was retired. On that evening, then Intercontinental Champion Rob Van Dam defeated then European Champion Jeff Hardy to unify the belts. The Euro title always seemed to be a rip-off of the more highly successful IC anyway.

PRETTY SAD DAY FOR THE HORSEMEN

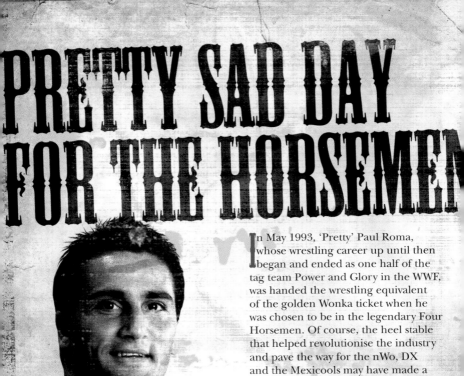

In May 1993, 'Pretty' Paul Roma, whose wrestling career up until then began and ended as one half of the tag team Power and Glory in the WWF, was handed the wrestling equivalent of the golden Wonka ticket when he was chosen to be in the legendary Four Horsemen. Of course, the heel stable that helped revolutionise the industry and pave the way for the nWo, DX and the Mexicools may have made a bigger mistake than in 1999 when the West Texas Rednecks opted to have Curly Bill join their group. It's only appropriate that the Ric Flair-led supergroup ran with the likes of the perennial mid-card pretty boy for a brief time because even the great Michael Jordan had to pass the ball sometimes. Speaking of which, you remember Dickey Simpkins, don't you?

The red-faced preaching gimmick was made famous by wrestling producer Bruce Prichard, whose infamous 'I love you' catchphrase was as in-your-face as Shawn Michaels throwing Marty Jannetty through the Barber Shop window or a defenceless good guy getting a handful of Fuji salt in the eyes. Love's berating of 80s heroes such as the Ultimate Warrior led to many memorable wrestling feuds. Love's biggest claim to wrestling fame was not his 15 minutes of WrestleMania

PLEASE STOP
THAT LOVING FEELING

glory with Morton Downey Jr., but as the first manager of the Undertaker. The controversial personality who preached 'the word of love' whenever he could was also part of another historic WWE debut in 1995, when his 'Brother Love Show' guest Ted DiBiase introduced the wrestling world to the Ringmaster, who eventually would become 'Stone Cold' Steve Austin.

5 SIDE SLAMMERS

FIVE UNSUNG HEROES IN THE *LAND OF 1,000 DANCES* VIDEO

1. Meatloaf
2. Vince McMahon
3. Uncle Elmer's Pig
4. Don Muraco
5. Paul Orndorff

MULKEY MANIA IS RUNNIN' WILD

Always on the losing end, the Mulkey Brothers were undoubtedly the worst tag team in the history of the wrestling business. The South Carolina natives made losing an art form during the height of the NWA's *World Championship Wrestling* programme on Saturday nights. The Mulkeys were the crap on the bottom of your shoe, while some might say they were the wrestling alternative to the NBA's lowly Clippers. Regardless of whether they are compared to a hot steaming pile of dog faeces or a second rate basketball team from Los Angeles is irrelevant; the bottom line is that the combination of Randy and Bill Mulkey meant it was a slam dunk victory for the opposing team.

Despite an abysmal record that had more losses than John Cena has Twitter followers, Mulkey Mania was born on March 28, 1987, when the blond bums managed to upset the Gladiators in the 'west coast champions' highly anticipated television debut. Much like the saying 'a snowball's chance in hell', the Mulkeys had finally beaten the odds and in the process earned an opportunity to compete in the coveted Jim Crockett Sr. Memorial Tag Team Tournament, only to lose to the team of Denny Brown and Chris Champion, whose claim to fame once upon a wrestling time was that he and his former New Breed partner Sean Royal were 'from the future'. Eventually gone the way of the buffalo, the stench left by Randy and Bill still resonates to this day and continues to linger like a bad Mulkey fart.

OWEN HART:
THE KING OF HARTS

To wrestling fans all over the world he was 'The King of Harts' and quite simply Owen Hart, the youngest sibling amongst wrestling royalty, had both the hardware and the reputation to prove it. After years of dabbling in and out of wrestling obscurity despite his untapped in-ring potential, the 'Black Hart' finally got his due when he turned his back on his family and began a feud with his Hall of Fame bro Bret 'Hitman' Hart. The two scientifically sound wrestling geniuses had several classic clashes, including a clean fall victory by Owen at WrestleMania X as well as that year's SummerSlam cage match that still stands as one of wrestling's greatest battles.

Despite being on the losing end during the majority of the feud with Bret, the former New Foundation member struck gold at WrestleMania XI when he teamed with his mystery partner Yokozuna and defeated the Smoking Gunns for the World Tag Team Championship. After several injuries left the high-flying Canadian on the shelf, he then started teaming with his brother-in-law Davey Boy Smith. With another tag title run in the books, tension between the two grapplers was evident until finally the Hitman intervened and stressed the importance of family, thus forming the anti-American Hart Foundation alongside the Bulldog, Bret, Jim 'The Anvil' Neidhart and long-time Hart buddy Brian Pillman.

The emergence of the heel-infused Hart Foundation also helped Owen to win singles gold. He captured the first of two Intercontinental titles at the expense of a pre-tooth fairy-ed Rocky Maivia. At SummerSlam '97, during a botched piledriver, Owen dropped Steve Austin on his head. Austin went on to win the match as planned despite the worst roll-up in wrestling history resulting in the worst T-shirt in wrestling history. Obviously, 'Owen 3:16' did not carry the same punch as the hugely popular 'Austin 3:16', thus a can of whupass was opened

and the injury-free 'Texas Rattlesnake' eventually re-claimed his gold on the same night as the now infamous 'Montreal Screwjob'.

When the 'Screwjob' smoke finally cleared Bret and his Foundation cronies (Anvil and Bulldog) were on their way to Atlanta, Georgia, home of the Nitro Party, while due to contract obligations Owen soon became WWE's 'Lone Hart'. Hart soon joined yet another powerful group, this time aligning with The Rock and D'Lo Brown as part of the 'Nation of Domination'. Soon however, the Nation began to disband and Hart began a tag team with Jeff Jarrett.

It was around this time that Hart also began appearing as the 'Blue Blazer', a masked superhero gimmick he once adopted during his initial WWE run years before his Bret back-stabbing ever began. The Blazer was re-introduced as the anti-Attitude era hero who also provided comic relief during most of his in-ring appearances.

On May 23, 1999, Hart, while dressed as the Blue Blazer, fell to his death performing a stunt prior to his scheduled match with Intercontinental Champion the Godfather as part of the now controversial Over the Edge pay-per-view. The next night on *Raw*, Hart's comrades, both in-ring friends and foes alike, paid tribute to a true wrestling warrior. At the following week's *Raw* event Jeff Jarrett captured the IC title that Hart was booked to win at Over the Edge, a clearly emotional victory dedicated to his highly respected partner but undoubtedly a match that will never fill the void left by the loss of his friend, the 'King of Harts'.

BLAME CANADA?

Before WCW closed up shop in Georgia, a viable heel stable was the Lance Storm-led Team Canada, which featured everyone from Elix Skipper to Mike Awesome. At one point, as we mentioned, WWE legend 'Hacksaw' Jim Duggan cut his long hair, shaved his beard and turned his back on the American flag. Long before that short-lived heel dump – we mean jump – Team Canada got instant heat led by stoic leader Storm, who captained a band of disgruntled Canadians

waging war on anything American for disrespecting his country. The gimmick worked but faded eventually (thanks, Duggan storyline) and was never picked up by WWE after they purchased WCW. Even so, a new Team Canada was created in 2004 on Total Nonstop Action Wrestling. This stable was short-lived as well – as it should be. We love Canada – the country has a great healthcare system and birthed the icon Rick Moranis.

HUG IT OUT

Just as storylines and gimmicks get recycled, wrestling moves do as well. How many wrestlers, for example, have used a variation of the 'powerbomb' as their finisher? The answer is a million billion. OK, that number is made up, but you get what we're saying. One move we don't see as often as we'd like to in the current wrestling climate is a good old-fashioned bear hug.

Back in the 1980s, we'd marvel as announcer Gorilla Monsoon would explain the severity of such a move (watch out sternum!) when it was

administered by such big men as Big John Studd and Andre the Giant. These days, however, the manoeuvre is a passing thing. With apologies to Chris Masters, it's mostly used as a precursor to a bigger, badder move. We long for the days where a bear hug was serious business – when it was explained to the audience as a career-ending, possibly life-ending move. So wrap your arms around an opponent today, future wrestling hall of famer! What the wrestling world needs today is a threat of death by man-love!

THE OTHER BRIAN ADAMS

In the pop world, Bryan Adams became a legend for recording delightfully cornball ballads that made ladies feel weak and men feel, um, uneasy. In the wrestling world, however, that name (spelled Brian Adams) resonated far more than excessive 'Everything I Do (I Do It For You)' airplay at weddings.

Like so many wrestlers, the Hawaiian got his start in the Land of the Rising Sun, and went on to have a lucrative career in wrestling under a few aliases. Adams was exposed to wrestling while serving in the military in Japan. Trained under Antonio Inoki, he made his debut in the states with Pacific Northwest Wrestling in the late 1980s under the moniker 'The Grappler'. Wrestling under a mask, Adams won that organisation's heavyweight championship before leaving for greener WWF pastures in 1990. There, he wrestled *sans* mask but with full-on make-up as Crush – the third member of highly successful tag champs Demolition. The effort to reinvigorate the face-painted tandem worked for a while but within roughly a year, Demolition disbanded and Adams returned to PNW.

photo:Wrealano@aol.com

After winning PNW's title again, Adams landed back in the WWF in 1992 – a terribly cheesy and somewhat uncreative period in McMahon company history. At a time when fake clowns interfered with real clowns' matches and cheesy neon outfits prevailed (hey, all of those applied to Adams), the wrestler made waves – pun intended – as the laid-back Hawaiian grappler Kona Crush. After notable feuds involving former Demolition tag team partner Barry Darsow (AKA Repo Man and Doink), Crush turned heel on former friend Randy Savage and battled him at WrestleMania X. Personal troubles (arrest due to alleged steroid/drug purchases) took Adams off TV for a while and he never really found a rightful place in the company again. A few gimmick changes, including a run as a member of the Nation of Domination, couldn't prevent him from leaving WWF for WCW in 1998.

As was the trend during the late 1990s, Adams found success wrestling under his own name for Ted Turner. He was a member of the nWo, and eventually won the Tag Team Championship titles twice as a member of the cooler-than-they-should've-been team KroniK with fellow big man Bryan Clark. When WWF purchased WCW, KroniK came along and feuded very briefly with the Undertaker and Kane. Following their release from WWF, they wrestled together in the AJPW. In the years leading up to his death, which was allegedly drug related, Adams dabbled in boxing with long-time friend Savage in his corner. Due to an injury, he had to bow out of his first match against Rick Zufal. Once that injury healed, he went back to wrestling but suffered a career-ending spinal injury in a 2003 match at the Tokyo Dome with Clark against Keiji Mutoh and Goldberg.

Looking back, Adams excelled in various incarnations in the business and was an under-appreciated talent. He even pulled off a mullet and those neon tights he wore as Crush, and that's saying something.

HAIL TO THE HIGH CHIEF

Before we smelled what the Scorpion King was cooking, Peter Maivia, The Rock's grandpa, was the first in the family to make time for tinsel town as he appeared in the 1967 James Bond film *You Only Live Twice*. Known as the 'Flying Hawaiian', the 'High Chief' was considered the head of the famous Samoan family which included his 'blood brothers' the Wild Samoans, the Tonga Kid, Umaga, Yokozuna and Rikishi.

'Uncle Peter' debuted in the WWE in 1977 along with a tough charismatic persona (sound familiar, Rock fans) and Samoan tribal tattoo. The real-life high chief fought the best the federation had to offer, and his patented Samoan drop would later be a signature part of The Rock's arsenal.

However, Maivia quickly became a hated grappler among fans because of his allegiance with 'Classy' Freddie Blassie and his heel turn on WWE mainstays Bob Backlund and Chief Jay Strongbow. His daughter married another popular star in the form of the 'Soulman' Rocky Johnson, thus literally planting the wrestling seeds for the arrival of the 'great one'.

Over the years the Samoan lineage has become a powerful bloodline among the wrestling heartbeat that lives true every time The Rock entertains the millions and millions of his fans all over the world. Since the High Chief's debut the Maivia and Anoa'i families respectively have been laying the smacketh down for years and years.

ARACHNOPHOBIA

Wrestling moves can sometimes feel like watching a re-run. Through the years, as we mentioned while discussing the beloved bear hug, manoeuvres can be slightly altered to create the lustre of a new wrestling innovation or re-used altogether – sorry Sheamus, but the Holy Cross isn't brand spanking new. In one case, however, that notion wasn't exactly the case.

Tajiri was a multi-talented wrestler in ECW and later in the WWE who shined on and off camera. If we can digress for a second, we miss the days of him serving as William Regal's assistant. The two very different wrestlers had a chemistry that so very few do, and didn't last as long as they should have together. In any event, the Japanese Buzzsaw was known mostly as a solid performer in the ring, delivering impressive kicks and flying around the squared circle. Sure, he made like Mr Fuji and spat green mist in opponents' eyes, but overall he was known for being utterly original. One instance of innovation was a move he mastered that no one will ever dare try to rip off – check that, they probably will. Using his body and the ropes to apply pressure to an opponent, Tajiri's Tarantula was one of the most unique and super-cool moves ever. It was also notable in that the wrestler could never earn a victory using this signature manoeuvre. Why? Um, not many wrestlers intentionally put their opponents anywhere near the ropes when they're using a submission move.

ROAD WARRIOR HAWK

DEMOLITION SCHMOLITION

He 'snacked on danger and dined on death' and for 20 years Michael Hegstrand, best known as Road Warrior Hawk, was one half of the greatest tag team that ever existed along with Joe 'Animal' Lauranaitis. The Legion of Doom, who grew up in Minnesota but were billed from Chicago, were paired up in 1983 with manager 'Precious' Paul Ellering by booker Ole Anderson. To look more imposing and bad ass the future Hall of Famers were dressed to the nines in spiked shoulder pads, face paint and dog collars resembling a no-nonsense duo straight off the set of *Mad Max 2: The Road Warrior*.

They destroyed the competition wherever they went. Starting off in Georgia and leading a path of destruction felt from Japan to the Minnesota-based American Wrestling Alliance (AWA), the Road Warriors were in-your-face and they were not afraid to back it up.

Eventually settling in the NWA, the award-winning tandem took on all comers including the Midnight Express, the Four Horsemen, and the Varsity Club, as well as Warrior knock-offs the Powers of Pain. Warlord and Barbarian matched LOD for power and even looks but they lacked greatly in the charisma department. They even fought the Russians – or, at least, that's what we were led to believe at the time. In fact, Krusher Krushchev was actually a role played by fellow Minnesota native and old training partner Barry Darsow.

Kicking NWA behinds was fun but soon the Road Warriors were in the WWE and they set their sights on becoming the first and only team to capture the tag team triple crown. Making quick work of Demolition (yet another bad imitation of the real deal), the LOD would soon re-introduce Paul Ellering to the loyal WWE fan base. Sadly the 'Precious One' was not alone, and Hawk would soon quit the federation, no thanks to a wooden puppet known as Rocco.

After a career-threatening injury to Animal and the Muppet miscue, Hawk soon found himself first wrestling solo in the independents as well as a brief go round in Japan as one half of the Hell Raisers with New Japan Pro Wrestling mid-carder Kensuke Sasaki. Despite a decent run Hawk would return to the United States and begin a programme in WCW, back with his Road Warrior brethren Animal by his side.

Trying to capture the magic of the old days, the masters of the Doomsday Device were re-packaged once again in WWE as Legion of Doom 2000, complete with blonde bombshell sidekick Tammy 'Sunny' Sytch. Not long after this a storyline was created that incorporated Hawk's real-life battles with drug and alcohol addiction that culminated in a 'suicidal' plunge from atop the *Monday Night Raw* TitanTron (the big screen).

After battling his demons and overcoming the effects of a heart condition that stopped him from competing in the ring, Hawk and Animal made a surprise appearance on *Raw* in May 2003. Five months later Michael Hegstrand was dead at the age of 46, passing in his sleep and leaving behind fond memories of the most successful tag team run in the history of the business… oooooh what a ruuuuuuuush!!!

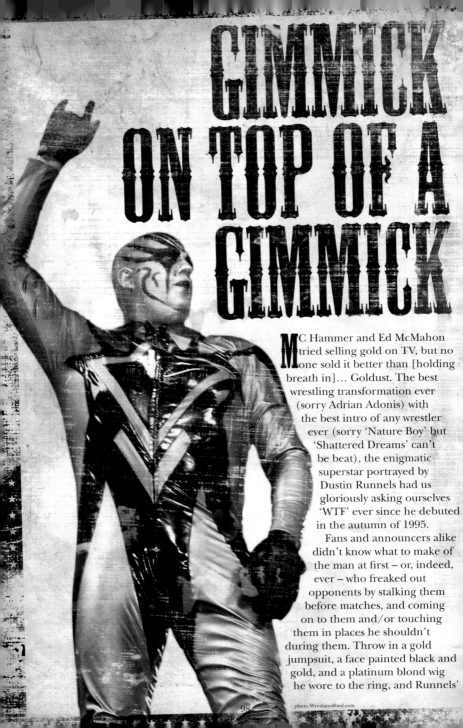

GIMMICK ON TOP OF A GIMMICK

MC Hammer and Ed McMahon tried selling gold on TV, but no one sold it better than [holding breath in]… Goldust. The best wrestling transformation ever (sorry Adrian Adonis) with the best intro of any wrestler ever (sorry 'Nature Boy' but 'Shattered Dreams' can't be beat), the enigmatic superstar portrayed by Dustin Runnels had us gloriously asking ourselves 'WTF' ever since he debuted in the autumn of 1995.

Fans and announcers alike didn't know what to make of the man at first – or, indeed, ever – who freaked out opponents by stalking them before matches, and coming on to them and/or touching them in places he shouldn't during them. Throw in a gold jumpsuit, a face painted black and gold, and a platinum blond wig he wore to the ring, and Runnels'

photo:Wrealano@aol.com

incarnation instantly became the most original heel of the 'Attitude' era or any era.

After a hiatus from the WWF (we'll omit the WCW years in-between), the former Intercontinental champ returned in his same rare form in 2001. Highlights from this comeback, which started with a great cameo appearance at the Royal Rumble, included a feud with Rob Van Dam, winning the Hardcore Championship multiple times, and teaming up with Booker T to form one of the funniest tag teams in WWE history. The odd couple ended up winning the Tag Team Championship before disbanding in 2003, and that brings us to the purpose of this segment.

Goldust clearly had the most original gimmick of all time when, in 2003, he was given yet another one. Following an attack by Batista and Randy Orton, who ended up electrically shocking him, the bizarre one developed a stutter and highly inappropriate form of Tourette's. Sure, it made for some great promos (notably anytime he crossed paths with 'Stone Cold' Steve Austin), but was it necessary to give a wrestler with a solid gimmick another gimmick? Pr-pr-pr-probably not. It was sort of like making the cast of *The Tap Dance Kid* learn the lambada halfway through its Broadway run.

GRAPPLING WITH MUSTACHES

Everyone has jumped on the mustache bandwagon in recent years – so much so it's hard to remember a time in which someone didn't blog about the fuzzy wonders or give out mock awards to a stache-certified star. Some people wrote books about the mustache craze before it became a renewed craze, but we digress. That brings us to this segment, which remembers a lost time in the wrestling world... a time in which upper-lip hair growth was part of the norm in the biz.

If you were to take a look at the best in the business in the 1970s–1990s,

chances are you'd stumble upon a mustache wearer. From Harley Race's connected face curls to Hulk Hogan's Twinkie fuzz to 'Ravishing' Rick Rude's porn stache, there was no better accessory for wrestlers of those eras than a pushbroom between the ropes. Nowadays, mustaches are grown to be hip or ironic, which is sad. Santino Marella is the only wrestler in the past two decades to sort of pull one off, but it was short-lived and too late in his run as a top funny face. Mustaches are meant to be worn – not worn out. Thanks hipsters.

YOKOZUNA:

SUMO ORIGATO

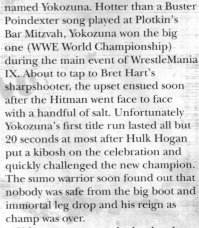

His first exposure for a major wrestling promotion in the United States was in the AWA wrestling as Kokina Maximus. However, Rodney Anoa'i's big break came in the form of one of the more larger-than-life characters to ever set foot in a WWE ring. Managed by Mr Fuji, the Samoan-born superstar was dubbed as a Japanese sumo wrestler

photo:Wrealano@aol.com

named Yokozuna. Hotter than a Buster Poindexter song played at Plotkin's Bar Mitzvah, Yokozuna won the big one (WWE World Championship) during the main event of WrestleMania IX. About to tap to Bret Hart's sharpshooter, the upset ensued soon after the Hitman went face to face with a handful of salt. Unfortunately Yokozuna's first title run lasted all but 20 seconds at most after Hulk Hogan put a kibosh on the celebration and quickly challenged the new champion. The sumo warrior soon found out that nobody was safe from the big boot and immortal leg drop and his reign as champ was over.

Yokozuna soon got the last laugh on Hogan and thanks to some more Fuji debauchery the monstrous heel regained the gold at the King of the Ring PPV in 1993. Yokozuna's storied career was soon highlighted by some classic encounters with the best of WWE's big men including the Undertaker, Vader and Earthquake.

Despite his untimely death in October 2000, the highly successful ring giant who was rather agile for his size was also a man of many firsts in regards to his storied wrestling career. As well as being the first heel champion to successfully defend his World Championship at a WrestleMania (X) he was also a part of the first and only casket match to be special enforced by 'Karate Kommando' Chuck Norris.

Sometimes actresses playing older women work. Right off the bat, Nicole Kidman's Oscar-winning turn in *The House* comes to mind as does Vicki Lawrence's captivating performance as Thelma Harper AKA 'Mama' of *Mama's Family*. But, sometimes it doesn't work, and in 2005, *Raw* came up lamer than the script to Cher's *Burlesque* movie.

2006. The role called for Momma to discipline and unleash her sass mouth every time her 'son' lost a match. The gimmick sort of worked in that the presence of his fake mother led to a strong heel turn from Benjamin, who went on to win the Intercontinental Championship over Ric Flair. He won the match thanks to drama from his mama. (She faked a heart attack and

BIG MOMMA'S RING

Shelton Benjamin was already an established athletic and high-flying superstar in WWE courtesy of Team Angle and solo success pre and post 'Money in the Bank' matches. His mic skills, however, lacked punch and higher-ups decided to bring in his loud and overbearing 'Momma', played by 1990s sitcom backwash Thea Vidale, in

distracted the ref.) Eventually, Vidale and her overlarge dresses wore out their welcome much like a Martin Lawrence *Big Momma* flick, and Benjamin trucked on as a solo act. While we applaud trying something new, we prefer Benjamin and any wrestler without the presence of an old bag.

WRESTLER RUN-IN
NIKOLAI VOLKOFF

'Bruno was always best in business to me and a true mentor.
Mic skills were tough for me because my English was never the best so that is why I had Freddie Blassie as my manager – the best manager ever. Freddie dying hit me hard because he was so close to me. I learned a great deal from him and miss him very much...My favourite gimmick is any gimmick that do good for business, if it can make money then it's a great gimmick.'

It was a phenomenon that hit its stride in the mid-90s, but slowly over the years it has become a lost art form. While most early adults were beginning to get their 'real' lives in order, everyone from the pre-pubescent kid next door to the already established thirty-something, backyard wrestling was not just a part-time job; it was a way of life.

Whether you were aspiring to be the next big star while reliving your childhood on an old torn mattress or you took advantage of your mum's old baking ware, chances are you were in some way, shape or form, affected by this untrained and unpredictable cult recreation.

Through home videos and the occasional missed spot, backyard wrestling was an underground hit among the most loyal and hardcore fans during professional wrestling's Monday Night Wars. It was a craze which was brought to the forefront with the help of hardcore legend Mick Foley, whose college exploits of jumping off of rooftops were immortalised on WWE television. Much like *Throw Momma from the Train* star Anne Ramsey it certainly wasn't a pretty sight, but regardless this collection of wrestling junkies got their fix through living out their dreams, all while gallivanting in mum and dad's backyard in their favourite wrestling singlet.

EXTREME ENTERTAINMENT?

DAMN KIDS

ANDY KAUFMAN:

INTER-GENDER WRESTLING CHAMPION OF THE WORLD

His obsession for pro wrestling was much larger than his size. However, what Andy Kaufman, the famous actor and entertainer, lacked in stature, he made up for with his willingness to take a bump as well as his elaborate plan to leave an indelible mark on the unpredictable world of sports entertainment.

He started proclaiming himself to be the 'Inter-Gender Wrestling Champion of the World' and soon his stage act was highlighted by nightly catfights with some very angry women who took Kaufman's boast very personally. The *Taxi* star even offered a $1,000 bounty to any woman who was able to pin his diminutive shoulders to the mat. Kaufman's famous foray into the squared circle was highlighted by his encounter with Memphis wrestling legend Jerry 'The King' Lawler.

The feud was centred around an in-ring showdown that resulted in a 'broken neck' for the Hollywood star and most notably the highly combustible squabble that ensued on a 1982 episode of *Late Night with David Letterman*. Appearing in a neck brace throughout his returning journeys into the Mid-South Coliseum along with Hall of Fame manager Jimmy Hart, along with a role in the 1983 film *My Breakfast with Blassie*, Kaufman's real-life effect on the business obviously helped set the stage for celebrity wrestling crossovers in the years and decades that followed.

Some of the greatest matches of all time featured bloodshed. We're not going to name them all but you know them. They typically happened during a main event cage match or a 'no DQ' battle between two stars. Sometimes, blood work got out of hand and didn't add much to matches. For example, in a Summerslam battle between icons Hulk Hogan and Shawn Michaels, HBK's blood kept flowing in a match that was way too slow-paced to match that outcome. In any event, that point is moot in the WWE lately.

Ever since Linda McMahon ran for office in 2010 (her loss was our loss), content on the company's *Raw* and *Smackdown* shows has been more geared to the PG crowd rather than the long-time PG-13 rating. John Cena is a champion kids can rally behind, but adults... um... not so much. And with Linda McMahon testing political waters, the company decided in 2010 to

THERE WON'T BE BLOOD

tone it down to benefit her campaign. The biggest casualty of this was bloody match outcomes. While TNA and Indy shows like Ring of Honor continue to 'juice', WWE has gone blood-free. We're not saying that all great matches end in blood but sometimes, when done right, the right amount of red flowing from an opponent's face can add such a deep impact. Case in point: would the Undertaker's match at WrestleMania X8 have been half as good had Ric Flair's head not become a piñata of red gob? Probably not.

CHIPS, DIP, AND A PITY PARTY

In the golden days of wrestling – when WCW battled WWF in the ratings during the mid-to-late 1990s – nothing seemed to stop the momentum of a show more than WCW's pointless Nitro Parties. In the middle of the action, WCW announcers Tony Schiavone and Bobby Heenan would cut away to one-time MTV personality Ricki Rachtman, who would be 'reporting' live from the house of a contest winner who had submitted footage of themselves and their friends having a party while watching *Monday Night Nitro*. Imagine how much effort this took in these pre-YouTube days. Anyway, Rachtman, along with the Nitro girls, would hang out with the winners – typically drunk frat boys eating nachos – and make it seem that we were all missing the party of the year. Obviously, we weren't. We were just missing some quality wrestling time.

Did we need Rachtman to show that wrestling fans are losers who stuff their faces and do shots every time the Demon enters the ring in Kiss facepaint on a weeknight? No. Every time Rachtman interrupted *Monday Night Nitro* made us feel how Mr Jefferson probably felt every time Harry Bentley rang his doorbell.

VINCE MCMAHON

PRESUMED DEAD

For as long as we can remember, *Saturday Night Live*, thanks to a skit centred around Toonces the Driving Cat, laid claim to the most comical and far-fetched car explosion on television. That was until the summer of 2007, when WWE ringmaster Mr McMahon was 'presumed dead' after his limo exploded outside a sold-out arena in Wilkes-Barre, Pennsylvania.

The June 11th *Raw* episode, which was actually billed as 'Vince McMahon Appreciation Night', was concluded by the fake death of the one-time Corporate Ministry's higher power. The federation which has had a penchant for pushing the envelope (insert Big Show riding a coffin being pulled by the Big Boss Man's hearse) even tried to insult our wrestling IQ by having us believe that the former ECW Champion was in fact in the limo during the explosion.

With the flag on the roof of WWE headquarters flying at half-mast to honour the perished leader of the XFL, the limo explosion angle itself was 'presumed dead' on the following week's *Raw* due to 'real life' circumstances that still haunt WWE to this day.

Of course the death of Vince went beyond appropriate even by wrestling standards, but when one lousy gimmick goes up in flames it's only right for it to be piggy-backed by one just as lame. Seriously, where else would you find a storyline that centres around a fake car explosion one week only to be followed up by the paternity suit heard round the wrestling world in which it was revealed that Vince McMahon's illegitimate long-lost child was actually a leprechaun? Hopefully history will not repeat itself anytime soon but regardless, it's obvious that Hornswoggle didn't benefit from the chairman's self-proclaimed balls the size of grapefruits.

ulk Hogan had his Hulkamaniacs, The Rock has his people and these days while Christian is backed by his peeps and Jeff Hardy is inspired by the creatures of the night, we can't help but remember a time when former Intercontinental and Hardcore Champion Andrew Martin was fuelled by the power of his Testicles. OK, for those of you keeping score at home, for wrestling personalities over the years it's been a rite of passage for many a popular star to name their respected fan base.

Martin debuted on an October 1998 episode of *Sunday Night Heat* as a bodyguard for Mötley Crüe. Soon enough the big man was aligning himself with The Rock and other Corporate heels, and thus Martin was simply known as Test. The Canadian-born star was later

SIDE SLAMMERS

10

FORGET TESTICLES, 10 FAN NAMES THAT SHOULD'VE CAUGHT ON

1. Harley Race's Race-ists
2. Funaki's Funbags
3. Earthquake's Aftershocks
4. Umaga's Amigos
5. The Missing Link's Sausage Links
6. Abdullah the Butcher's Prime Ribs
7. Bad News Brown Nosers
8. Matt Hardy's DWIs
9. One Man Gang Bangers
10. Glacier's Icicles

NICE TEST (ICLES)

removed from the Corporation and soon found allegiance with the Union; a face stable at the time that was rebelling against the McMahon-infused bad boys of the WWE.

Test's greatest push was during an on-air relationship-turned-sour-grapes with Stephanie McMahon, which helped usher in the McMahon–Helmsley era but quickly buried the heartbroken star into tag team obscurity. Sprinkle in a few solo and tag team title reigns and a brief run as a member of both T & A and the Un-Americans, and Test's career as a solid in-ring performer was right on the money. Seriously, how many wrestlers can claim they were good enough to have 'Big Poppa Pump' Scott Steiner reluctantly become their personal manservant?

Backed by his legion of faithful Testicles, one of Test's last hurrahs was a brief stint as a ruthless no-nonsense villain in the watered-down WWE version of ECW and finally in TNA as the 'Punisher' Andrew Martin, aligning himself with Orlando regulars Sting and Abyss.

Upon his in-ring retirement and untimely death, the master of the pumphandle slam will be remembered as a physically intimidating presence that carved out a decent run as well as holding his own during the highly combustible Attitude era. But seriously, since we are on that topic, WTF is a Kananite anyway?

Siskel & Ebert made their mark in pop culture history by giving 'two thumbs' up or down for movies they saw. By comparison, in the history of wrestling, no other grappler made his mark using his first digit more than Umaga. The wrestler's 'Samoan Spike' to an opponent's throat debilitated them more than any Pauly Shore movie did to Gene and Roger. But, the man born Edward Fatu was so much more than a quick thumb shot.

Born into the iconic Anoa'i wrestling family, Fatu's career path was likely set from the womb on. Trained by his uncles Afa and Sika and wrestling as one half of the Island Boyz and other similarly-themed gimmicks, it didn't take long for the large and surprisingly agile talent to land on WWE television. In 2002, he debuted as Jamal – one half of the lethal tag team 3-Minute Warning along with his real-life cousin Rosey (Matt Anoa'i). The tag team, brought on TV by then-*Raw* general manager Eric Bischoff, disseminated opponents in under three minutes, and had a very strong year which included breaking up the infamous Billy and Chuck wedding. Surprisingly, the team disbanded prematurely when Fatu was released after roughly a year. After stints in TNA and All Japan Pro Wrestling, he resurfaced in the WWE in 2005 under a new gimmick and a whole lot of face paint.

With Samoan tattoos all over his face and body, Fatu became Umaga, a crippling freight train who squashed his opponents with various signature moves including the aforementioned Spike and Wild Samoan splash. Umaga never spoke – instead he had his manager – the ever-so-annoying Armando Alejandro Estrada – talk trash on his behalf. During his Goldberg-

esque run, Umaga went undefeated for nearly nine months, and won matches against such opponents as Ric Flair and Kane. He also feuded with Triple H and challenged (but lost for the first time to) John Cena for the WWE Championship.

Umaga's shining moment – next to winning the Intercontinental Championship twice – would come at WrestleMania XXIII, where he was featured in the main event as part of the 'Battle of the Billionaires'. That night, Umaga represented Vince McMahon against one-hit-wonder Bobby Lashley, representing Donald Trump, in a Hair vs. Hair match. While Umaga ended up losing and McMahon's head was shaved bald, he remained a top heel in the company for quite some time – even after he was defeated by then-unknown Santino Marella for the Intercontinental belt (he'd eventually win it back).

During his final months at WWE, Umaga took part in many key matches at key PPVs but lost each time out. He fell to Batista at WrestleMania XXIV, and lost to Jeff Hardy at the One Night Stand PPV. By 2009, he was drafted to *Smackdown* and had a significant feud with CM Punk in that it marked the first time Umaga ever uttered a word on camera. As was the case in his first incarnation in WWE, Fatu was released from the company when he failed a drug test and allegedly refused to go to rehab.

In November 2009, Umaga wrestled on Hulk Hogan's Hulkamania tour in Australia until his death on December 4 of that year of a heart attack. While his time on this planet was short, Fatu made the most of a wrestling career that would get two thumbs up from any wrestling critic.

It had no reason to work. The fans shouldn't have eaten it up as much as they did. Yet, the idea of having a wrestler with a superhero gimmick got 'over' so well for Gregory Shane Helms. As 'The Hurricane', Helms entertained kids and adults and made wrestling fans forget all about his previous gimmick as a member of WCW's 3-Count.

Helms started wrestling as 'The Hurricane' in the summer of 2001, and instantly won the European Championship over Matt Hardy. Eventually, he started teaming with the super stoic Lance Storm, and formed a solid bond with Molly Holly who was rebranded as his spunky sidekick 'Mighty Molly'. The pair, who hilariously rode to the ring in 'The Hurri-Cycle', fought crime… we mean opponents, in the WWE until Molly hit her partner with a frying pan to capture the Hardcore title at WrestleMania X8.

The Hurricane would go on to be a very successful gimmick for Helms with or without Holly. His super gimmick was surely a highly profitable marketing move for the WWE who sold masks, shirts and foam fingers for their superstar. Through the years, Hurri-Helms would go on to win the Cruiserweight belt, and share the World Tag Team Titles with unlikely partner Kane (the Hurri-Kane – get it?). Despite years of success, his crowning achievement was likely defeating The Rock in a 2003 episode of *Raw*. (The Rock was distracted by future WrestleMania opponent 'Stone Cold' Steve Austin.)

NO MORE SUPERHEROES IN WRESTLING?
WHAT'S UP WIT DAT?

Another key to his men-in-tights run was forming a tag team with 3-Minute Warning's Rosey. Many priceless television moments were made with The Hurricane training Rosey to be a superhero, and to a lesser degree, with 'Super Stacy' Keibler, who joined the tag team for some much needed adult-cred and eye candy. After a solid run of well over a year, the tandem of Rosey and The Hurricane came to an end when Helms took off his mask and turned heel.

After years of success as an unmasked tough guy, Helms returned in the autumn of 2008 with his Hurricane gimmick. Who could forget his 'I'm just sayin' catchphrase when posing as ace reporter Gregory Helms, which almost made us forget about his funny 'What's up wit dat' tag line as The Hurricane. The Hurricane has been off TV for a while, which brings us up to the whole reason for this entry: bring him back. As Bonnie Tyler once sang, we're 'holding out for a hero!'

photo: Matt Roberts

ONE... BUT NOT THE SAME

It happened once a year, but unlike Christmas, it didn't really make us giddy with excitement – at least not as much as it had. It was the WWE Draft, a night in which the company's *Raw* and *Smackdown* (no, not ECW anymore) select stars from the other brand's roster at 'random'. The draft had been huge in changing the scenery and course of a show (John Cena's draft from *Smackdown* to *Raw* is legendary whether you like him or not), but we long for the days where *Raw* and *Smackdown* use the entire WWF/WWE roster for both shows consistently and, more importantly, had one championship title for both shows.

This hasn't been the case since the WWE launched its brand extension in 2002, and it's time for it to return. Just as the draft became tired, having champs per show has as well. Let's have one roster and one brand of titles for all WWE programming – now there's something Funaki can get behind.

BAD NEWS,

Meaner than a junkyard dog and more unpredictable than an M. Night Shyamalan crappy film ending, Bad News Brown was one of the best heels in WWF/WWE history despite being with the company for a brief tenure.

Born Allen James Coage, the New York native first gravitated to heavyweight judo before battling opponents in the wrestling ring. In the mid-to-late 1970s, a time in which eventual *Karate Kid* star Pat Morita was working behind the *Happy Days* diner counter, Coage perfected his craft and became a martial arts master. A US Grand Champion in judo, he took home the Olympic bronze medal in 1976. Despite years of kicking people harder than Kung-Fu Panda, Coage eventually traded judo chops for body slams in 1978.

After debuting on the Indy circuit (he made a pit stop at the WWF) and grappling in New Japan, Coage made his mark in the wrestling Mecca of

Calgary. There, he wrestled for Stu Hart's Stampede Wrestling and stayed there for most of the 1980s. By 1988, however, he returned to the WWF, only this time wrestling under the moniker Bad News Brown. As Brown, his approach and attitude was to destroy anyone who got in his way – no matter who they were. This notion made him a multidimensional heel who took out other heels who got in his way, (for example, he eliminated Bret Hart to win the WrestleMania IV battle royal), faces, and even fake presidents. Who could forget when he attacked Jack Tunney in an infamous 'Brother Love' episode because he wasn't given 'number one contender' status?

In his two-plus years at the WWF, Brown feuded with everyone from Randy Savage to Hulk Hogan (you remember that *Saturday Night's Main Event* match, don't you?), and took on Jake 'The Snake' Roberts in a nonsensical sewer rat versus snake match. Coage left the company in 1990, supposedly because he felt

GOOD WRESTLER

underutilised and never claimed gold. He wrestled independently until his retirement in 1999, and died of a heart attack on March 6, 2007. While he never captured a championship, Brown remains one of the most memorable heels and demands our respect. He paved the way for future unpredictable stars like 'Stone Cold' Steve Austin, and for that, his legacy is pretty bad ass.

In 1988 Ted Turner purchased the rights to World Championship Wrestling and from 1995 until its dramatic demise in 2001, the once prominent promotion that aspired to be 'where the big boys play' was just another victim to fall at the hands of Vince McMahon and the WWE Empire. Whether it was backstage politics, television overexposure, the emergence of the No Limit Soldiers or quite possibly the inability to push new faces while continuing to shine the spotlight on the stars of yesterday, no one really knows for sure what led to the demise of WCW. Call it what you will but the

On April 24, 2000, Arquette pinned Bischoff on *Monday Nitro,* and two days later the *Scream* star and former Mr Courtney Cox won the WCW World Championship while teaming with Diamond Dallas Page against Jeff Jarrett and Bischoff. The stipulation of the match called for the man who scored the winning pin to become the new champion. To his credit, Arquette was against winning the title that was never won by wrestling legends such as Jake 'The Snake' Roberts or 'Rowdy' Roddy Piper. It should also be noted that all the dough he made during his historical publicity stunt turned WCW disaster was donated to the families of Owen Hart, Brian Pillman and Darren Drozdov, surely a classy move by the most undeserving champion of all time.

DAVID ARQUETTE:

WRESTLING WITH THE STARS

final nail in the Turner-led coffin will forever be linked to the rise and very hard fall of one very undeserving World Heavyweight Champion – David Arquette.

After the release of the un-critically acclaimed movie *Ready to Rumble,* actor David Arquette was brought into storylines and thrust quickly into the ring to confront company figurehead Eric Bischoff and the newly-formed New Blood stable. (On a side note we would pay top dollar for one of those Hogan approved F.U.N.B. tees, just saying.)

Before he ever uttered wrestling's most iconic catchphrase in front of Michael 'P.S.' Hayes and the entire world, Steve Austin was left for not in squared circle Siberia clamouring for a chance to rewrite the history books and make us all quickly forget about 'The Ringmaster'.

THE LEGEND OF CHILLY MCFREEZE

The 'psalms' Austin dropped on that crowning night at the 1996 King of the Ring at Jake 'The Snake' Roberts' expense no less ushered in a new era for an industry that had certainly seen much brighter days. It was essentially Austin's, 'so whatcha gonna do' and unfortunately it almost never happened.

Legend has it that after Austin ditched manager Ted DiBiase and his original WWE gimmick he was given creative freedom on what to do next in regards to his character's future. It was understood that Austin's next career move was going to be loosely based on a 'natural born killer' with blood as cold as ice, and yes, the name Chilly McFreeze was given some thought. The 'Stone Cold' name, crazily enough, was created over a cup of tea shared between the wrestler turned action movie star and his ex-wife Jeannie Clark. No way does Austin become the beer-guzzling, boss-defying Texas rattlesnake with a name like Chilly McFreeze. Thankfully cooler heads prevailed, but let's be honest – if they didn't and 'Stone Cold' never sees the light of day then the Attitude era never happens and we would still be living in a Doink-induced world, and that's the bottom line.

10 SIDESLAMMERS

TEN SIGNS WCW WAS GOING UNDER

1. David Arquette wins the gold
2. LWO forms
3. Even Dean Malenko left
4. David Flair
5. Martin Landau cast in *Ready to Rumble*
6. The Giant takes the plunge
7. Master P and the No Limit Soldiers invade *Monday Nitro*
8. Glacier is given the ball on *Thursday Thunder*
9. Booker T becomes G.I. Bro
10. The Fake Sting joins the nWo

Michael Cole has done a great job of late as a misguidedly confident wrestling announcer who ventures into the ring, but no one did it better than the delightfully annoying Jonathan Coachman, AKA 'The Coach'. The former wrestling colour commentator, manager, whipping boy and terrible wrestler shined for nearly a decade as the straight-laced Carlton Banks-ish voice of many a WWE broadcast.

A former basketball star in college and sports reporter, Coachman started working for WWF/WWE in December 1999 as a commentator, backstage interviewer, and wide receiver… of jokes

former *Heat* announcer viciously made fun of the tandem of Jerry Lawler and Jim Ross, and went on to compete in forgettable wrestling matches that he won usually by a special run-in.

Among Coach's other highlights were joining Lawler and Ross briefly in the *Raw* broadcast booth, taking on Batista in a lop-sided loss at Taboo Tuesday, being a participant in the 2006 Royal Rumble, and graduating from Mr McMahon's executive assistant to the consistently replaceable Raw's interim general manager.

By 2008, after years in and out of the ring and always reporting from

FLYING COACH

at his expense. Many of Coachman's finest moments came opposite The Rock, who delivered machine-gun insults and convinced him to make an ass out of himself by either singing or dancing.

Like the aforementioned Cole, Coachman really came into his own by the early 2000s when he went heel. As Eric Bischoff's second banana, the

the squared circle sidelines, Coachman left WWE for his dream job as a sports reporter/anchor for ESPN. While he's at the Sports Center desk now, and has traded in one Connecticut city for another (Stamford in favour of Bristol), we miss the walking gimmick that was Jonathan 'The Coach' Coachman. Cole can try, but there can be only one Coach.

10

SIDE SLAMMERS

10 WITH BEST MIC SKILLS EVER

1. Ric Flair
2. Stone Cold Steve Austin
3. Jake The Snake Roberts
4. The Rock
5. Macho Man Randy Savage
6. Roddy Piper
7. Raven
8. Santino Marella
9. Hollywood Hogan
10. CM Punk

RAVING LUNA-TIC

Provocative and suggestive ring attire. Bras and panties matches. *Playboy* and *Maxim* cover shoots. Yep, the presence of female wrestlers seems more for eye candy than in-ring accolades. In the rarest cases, however, they're viewed as competent competitors and no one excelled in this 'man's world' more than Luna Vachon. Sorry, Chyna.

With an intimidating look, physique, and a much deeper and scarier voice than the *Masters of the Universe*'s Evil-Lyn, Vachon was an intense wrestling presence that just happened to be female. Born in Canada, Vachon (born Gertrude) was surrounded by wrestling with her Aunt Vivian, step-dad Paul 'Butcher' and Uncle 'Mad Dog' hitting the ropes for a living and her godfather being the one and only Andre the Giant. Fittingly, she trained in her teens with Aunt Viv and the Fabulous Moolah and made her professional debut in the mid-1980s by competing in Florida Championship Wrestling. There, she honed her skills and outlandish looks – shaving half her head as part of a storyline with Kevin Sullivan.

After stints in POWW, the AWA, and Stu Hart's Stampede Wrestling – in the latter of which she managed the Blackheart tandem of ex-husband Tom Nash and future husband David Heath – she joined the WWF. By 1993, she was thrown right into a major feud in the WWF, debuting at WrestleMania IX as Shawn Michaels' new valet in a match against Tatanka, who was escorted to the ring by former Michaels handler Sensational Sherri.

Eventually, Vachon moved on from the feud with Sherri and allegiance to the Heartbreak Kid, and partnered with a smitten Bam Bam Bigelow. The Beast from the East was so in love with her he even changed the name of his signature

Moonsault to the Lunasault. In any event, the unique pair, who didn't win any beauty contests by the way, went on to many successes in the lacklustre Doink era.

Eventually, she left the company over alleged creative differences, and returned to the Indy circuit and eventually ECW as Tommy Dreamer's valet. In 1997, she arrived in WCW ever so briefly and returned to the WWF later in the year and arguably found her biggest professional success. Over the next few years, she'd compete against the top women's champions, and even a few male champs along the way. In arguably her most memorable stint at WWF, she teamed with Goldust, creating a wonderfully strange tandem that eventually took on far prettier power couple Marc Mero and Sable at WrestleMania.

She and her husband Gangrel, who she managed, eventually left the WWF for the Indy circuit. She would eventually retire from the business and on August 27, 2010, was found dead of an accidental drug overdose. While she failed to win any gold in the WWF, Vachon ranks as one of the most influential female wrestlers of our time. What other female wrestler can say they competed in a steel cage match against a man (Stevie Richards in ECW), wrestled in a hardcore match against a woman (Ivory in the WWF), and defeated a Gillberg?

photo: Tim Harshman

Whether he made you laugh, cry or cheer, one thing is for certain: 'Latino Heat' made sure you got your money's worth every time he stepped into the ring. Admired by fans and peers alike, Eddie Guerrero's legacy among the gods is that of a true warrior who helped pave the way for international stars to shine throughout the wrestling world.

Eddie's first big break occurred as a member of Los Gringos Locos along with fellow American-born wrestler Art Barr (yes that's right, The Juicer from WCW was just name-dropped). They formed a tag team that was despised done, none stood out more than his memorable bouts against Dean Malenko under the South Philly lights.

In 1995 Guerrero made the switch to WCW, appearing in that year's World War 3 60-man Battle Royal, making it all the way to the final nine. The future United States Champion would help put the Cruiserweight division on the map with the help of such stars as the already mentioned Malenko, Chris Jericho, Syxx, Rey Mysterio Jr. and yes, even you, 'Das Wunderkind'. As his popularity was rising Guerrero and other similar stars, especially those of 'Latino' descent, began to

EDDIE GUERRERO

LONG LIVE THE LASSO FROM EL PASO

across Mexico, a hatred that landed them a headlining match during AAA's first ever pay-per-view in the States, called 'When Worlds Collide'. The Crazy Americans lost their 'Hair vs. Mask' match to El Hijo del Santo and Octagon. It was during this time that the duo caught the eye of ECW owner Paul Heyman and he soon offered them a chance to reach new heights in the land of extreme.

Sadly, Barr never made it to Philadelphia, passing away before he could join Guerrero in ECW. The El Paso native quickly proved himself to be a major player and in his first match in wrestling's most famous Bingo Hall he captured the ECW World Television Title from 2 Cold Scorpio. With many classic showdowns that ended up on his résumé before it was all said and

show frustration towards company figurehead Eric Bischoff and the idea that the WCW president refused to push certain wrestlers to be main event stars – and thus, the Latino World Order was formed.

The LWO was short-lived, however, after Guerrero was involved in a serious car accident. In a few months he would return to the WCW ring as a member of the Filthy Animals, but sooner rather than later, Eddie was given his release from the company and the next chapter in his wrestling life would begin in the next millennium as a member of World Wrestling Entertainment. Along with other former WCW talent (Malenko, Benoit and Perry Saturn), the Radicalz made their cohesive debut on a shocking episode of *Monday Night Raw*.

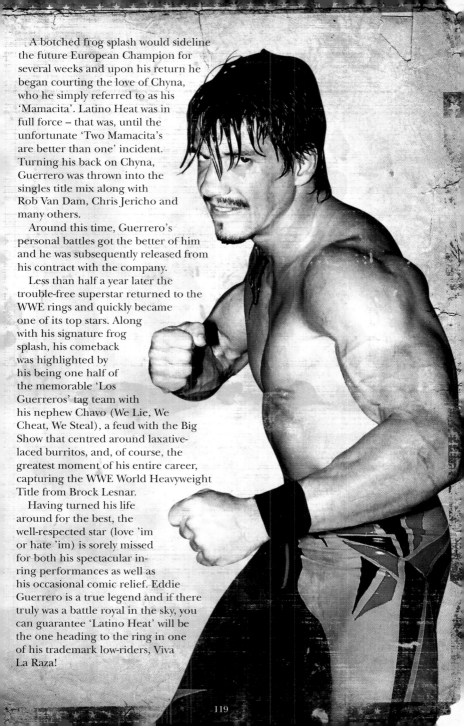

A botched frog splash would sideline the future European Champion for several weeks and upon his return he began courting the love of Chyna, who he simply referred to as his 'Mamacita'. Latino Heat was in full force – that was, until the unfortunate 'Two Mamacita's are better than one' incident. Turning his back on Chyna, Guerrero was thrown into the singles title mix along with Rob Van Dam, Chris Jericho and many others.

Around this time, Guerrero's personal battles got the better of him and he was subsequently released from his contract with the company.

Less than half a year later the trouble-free superstar returned to the WWE rings and quickly became one of its top stars. Along with his signature frog splash, his comeback was highlighted by his being one half of the memorable 'Los Guerreros' tag team with his nephew Chavo (We Lie, We Cheat, We Steal), a feud with the Big Show that centred around laxative-laced burritos, and, of course, the greatest moment of his entire career, capturing the WWE World Heavyweight Title from Brock Lesnar.

Having turned his life around for the best, the well-respected star (love 'im or hate 'im) is sorely missed for both his spectacular in-ring performances as well as his occasional comic relief. Eddie Guerrero is a true legend and if there truly was a battle royal in the sky, you can guarantee 'Latino Heat' will be the one heading to the ring in one of his trademark low-riders, Viva La Raza!

Bobby 'The Brain' Heenan was a pure wrestling genius, whether he was dishing out insults to ringside fans that he mockingly referred to as 'humanoids' or openly dissing the boys in the back as 'ham-and-eggers'. Over the years the 'broadcast journalist' knew how to draw heat better than anyone in the business and his on-screen banter with Gorilla Monsoon swiftly became the stuff of legend. And so it makes complete sense that the legendary 'Weasel' was thrust front and centre into the most unwatchable feud in wrestling history.

known as the cigar-smoking, torn Yankee shirt-wearing Brooklyn Brawler.

Although Heenan's Hall of Fame credentials and his occasional Weasel suit donning could not save this feud, the Rooster–Brawler war is certainly one for the ages. This anti-climactic showdown of wrestling's premiere jobbers may or may not have put the Rooster's 'Cock of the Walk' sharpshooter on the map but it also helped land former 'Knuckleball' throwing pitcher turned wrestler Abe Schwartz a brief stint on *Monday Night Raw*.

BATTLE OF THE HAM-AND-EGGERS

In 1988, former NWA star Terry Taylor was given the now infamous WWF 'rebrand' and quickly became wrestling's first and only 'Red Rooster'. The Taylor makeover was rewarded with a slot among the Heenan Family elite but soon deteriorated when Dick the Bruiser's worst enemy (Heenan) began demeaning the former NWA Television Champion, resulting in the most lop-sided WrestleMania showdown this side of a King Kong Bundy elbow drop on a helpless Little Beaver. His 30-second squash during the fifth installment of wrestling's greatest show on earth resulted in a face turn for Taylor and his infamous rooster comb and, more importantly, culminated in a brief and never-really-settled feud with long-time WWE employee turned occasional scrub wrestler Steve Lombardi, who was better

photo:Wrealano@ac

The Mighty Mighty Bosstones are a great ska band out of Boston who released a bunch of danceable punk hits like 'The Impression That I Get' and 'Where Did You Go?' While we enjoyed listening to and sometimes moshing to the band, one thing that struck us more was how their best asset didn't even play an instrument or sing a note. Yep, Ben Carr was the band's dancer and he added so much by saying nothing at all.

That's the sort of guy Mike Jones was in the 1980s and 1990s in wrestling. Never a main event threat or a chatty Cathy, the man who performed in the WWF as Virgil shined by simply standing by the 'Million Dollar Man' Ted DiBiase and always watching his back. Long before WWF gave him his shot at fame as DiBiase's bodyguard, Jones wrestled independents under the name Soul Train Jones. Since that name sounded like a terrible disco ball era gimmick, he became Lucius Brown in the WWF.

The duo traded the Million Dollar Title back and forth but once their feud was over, Virgil was relegated to low-card matches. In 1996, Jones joined WCW under the name Vincent – a take on Vince McMahon – and became the nWo's head of security. Much as he did for DiBiase, Jones let his muscles do most of the talking throughout this run, which included two more name changes, by the way (Shane and Mr Jones).

Jones retired from the business in the early 2000s and became a teacher. He still makes wrestling appearances, however, returning as Virgil on a 2010 episode of *Raw* working alongside Ted DiBiase, Jr. While the gimmick of having another wrestler serve as a bodyguard for a talent and eventual foe (think Alex Riley and The Miz), we miss the days where a valet could get by on actions alone. We also miss the days where competing companies could create characters as a slap in the face to one another. On a related note, we'd look

A THOUSAND DOLLAR MAN

By 1987, however, Jones was renamed Virgil – a moniker supposedly given to him as a knock against Dusty Rhodes, whose real name is Virgil Runnels. Virgil held all of DiBiase's assets and whenever DiBiase ran for cover against an opponent it was usually his bodyguard who got the brunt of an ass-whipping.

After four years plus together, Virgil eventually turned on DiBiase and fought him at WrestleMania VII and SummerSlam.

forward to Virgil making a comeback as much as we look forward to christening a pair of cute flannel pj bottoms for the first time of the Christmas season.

photo:Wrealano@aol.com

With his distinct voice, 80s combover and 'stache, Howard Finkel was as synonymous with wrestling as some of the biggest stars were of the 1980s and 1990s. With the company since its inception, 'The Fink' has been an integral part of the company mostly for his work announcing matches (notably at Madison Square Garden) from the mid-to-late 1970s through the 2000s. He also reportedly helped behind

photo:Wrealano@aol.com

THE MISSING FINK

the scenes, assisting in storylines, and coming up with the name WrestleMania and some wrestlers' gimmicks.

But it's announcing where Fink became legend. As kids of the 1980s, who didn't love hearing Finkel unleash '…and NEW World Heavyweight Champion…' after a title changed hands? We all did, and Fink as ring announcer was one of the most successful gimmicks in wrestling history. But since 2000, the man with a voice

more crisp than Casey Kasem after an hour of vocal warm-ups hasn't had a lot of face time. Instead, he's kept backstage and has been replaced by younger and sometimes prettier ring announcers.

While Lillian Garcia was nice to look at, we'd rather watch Finkus Maximus in a tux ready to pop the crowd. It's time for him to return to the ring. We miss him announcing and, somewhat surprisingly, long for him to take part in storylines and matches. Who could forget when he took on Harvey Wippleman in his tighty whities on *Raw*? Or the time he helped X-Pac shave Jeff Jarrett's head? Or lastly, the time he took on Garcia in a tuxedo/evening gown match to claim lead announcer status?

We could go on, but we'll cut to the chase. There's a reason the man once dubbed 'El Dopo' is in the WWE Hall of Fame. He's the guy you want introducing the number one match. Suck it, Michael Buffer.

'Have you seen my wiener?'

That's a memorable line that was delivered by Cameron Diaz's character's special needs brother in the comedy classic *There's Something About Mary*. The depiction of the lovably annoying Warren ('franks and beans') was hilarious but probably came under fire from various groups since the actor who played him wasn't handicapped. We wonder what they said about Eugene. Lord knows we cringed every time he entered the ring or cut a promo. More on that in a second…

In the history of the WWE/WWF, there have been a fair number of wrestlers who were a few fries short of a Happy Meal. The Bushwackers were clearly a bit off. Al Snow talked to a mannequin head, and hoisted it up on his way to and inside the ring. We won't even bother elaborating on this point, but if you're curious, Google the Oddities or Festus. In any event, in 2004, for the first time and likely last time ever in the company's history, the WWE had the audacity to debut another clueless, easily manipulated grappler who happened to have special needs. Eugene, portrayed by the fully-functioning Nick Dinsmore, debuted on *Raw* as then-general manager Eric Bischoff's handi-capable nephew.

What amazed us about Eugene – beside the fact how over he got and how kind of sorta wrong the whole gimmick was in the first place – was just how long the special little guy lasted in the company and the greats he shared face time with. In his tenure at WWE, he

WELL ISN'T THAT SPECIAL

managed to win the tag belts with William Regal, feuded with main eventers like Triple H and Umaga, won Kurt Angle's gold medals, and got icons The Rock and Hulk Hogan to get his back. Speaking of the latter, who could forget when the Hulkster came to Eugene's defence when Muhammed Hassan and Daivari attacked him? Off topic, how Eugene managed a 'Mania moment while Bischoff did not is one of the greatest mysteries of all time.

Eugene's appeal eventually went away – we're pretty sure he wore a cape to the ring in his final days – but he had a solid run. That said, for us, there just wasn't anything really special about him at all.

Most wrestlers will tell you that their in-ring personas are simply exaggerated, ramped up versions of themselves. Well, most will. Don't ask Doink or Disco Inferno that question. In the case of Ray Traylor, who started his career as a prison guard, that notion rang true.

The big man, who died of a heart attack in 2004 at just 41 years old, left Georgia inmates behind in favour of a wrestling career in the mid-1980s, debuting in WCW under his real name and taking off as Jim Cornette's bodyguard Big Bubba Rogers. Rogers feuded for quite some time with the 'American Dream' Dusty Rhodes, who reportedly came up with Traylor's new gimmick, and eventually won the Universal Wrestling Federation title before leaving for greener pastures in 1988 with the WWF.

Repackaged as the Big Boss Man, Traylor became a top heel, drawing heat courtesy of his fast-talking manager Slick, and adding insult to injury when he defeated an opponent by handcuffing them to the ropes and beating them with his nightstick after he pinned them. Among his many highlights – in his first WWF run – were attacking Hulk Hogan on a 'Brother Love' episode, which led to an all-out feud which culminated in steel cage matches he'd end up losing. While he was a strong presence in singles matches, Boss Man took off as well in tag action. Matched with former WCW foe One Man Gang, who went all Akeem on us, the pair took on just about everyone in tag competition from the Mega Powers to Demolition.

The tag team would eventually go the way of Sonny and Cher (Boss Man handily beat Akeem at WrestleMania VI), but Traylor remained a force in the WWF even after he turned face. Eventually, he'd leave the WWF in favour of WCW. There, he wrestled as the Guardian Angel and his Big Bubba Rogers character before turning face and taking his WCW career full circle by grappling under his given name.

In 1999, Traylor returned as the Boss Man in the WWF and excelled

CARRY A BIG STICK

photo: Wrealano@aol.com

in tag action. He won the Tag Team Championship with fellow Corporation member Ken Shamrock, and won the Hardcore Championship as well. He memorably took on the Undertaker in a Hell in a Cell match at WrestleMania XV, and despite that loss, it resonated far more than a series of odd gimmick matches he'd eventually have. Who could forget when he got in a battle over Al Snow's dog Pepper (Kennel from Hell match, anyone?), and stole the Big Show's father's coffin. Let's give him a mulligan for those latter storylines and focus on what a big, bad and arresting presence he was in the wrestling world.

WRESTLING WITH ATTITUDE

CLOTHING OPTIONAL

Scantily clad babes, rebellious anti-heroes and a penchant for pushing the envelope: this is what defined the Attitude era, the WWE's risk-taking stretch of borderline R-rated programming that helped breathe new life into an industry that so desperately needed a change from the over-the-top cartoon characters that consumed its existence.

They told us to 'suck it' and to 'know your role' and they even taught us how to flip the bird in the face of authority. The Attitude era was filled with its share of controversy, beer drinking and plenty of crotch chopping to go around so it's no wonder that Dennis Knight, a mid-carder at best (e.g. Tex Slazenger, Phineas I. Godwinn), was able to portray a character that personified the true essence of the most provocative era in the history of pro wrestling.

In 1998, after years of service as an evil pig farmer, Knight was 'kidnapped' and soon joined up with the Undertaker's Ministry of Darkness. Repackaged as 'Mideon', the former two-time Tag Team Champion became the WWE European Champion after finding the hardware in Shane McMahon's bag. (So that's how the Euro title lost its remaining credibility.)

Anyway, after two years of middling around doing the Deadman's dirty work, Knight began a programme as a Mankind imitator. Unfortunately the fake Foley had as much impact on *Raw* as Jason the Sexiest Man Alive had on the extreme masses in the ECW arena. In 2000, several months after Dick Clark's Y2K celebration, WWE dropped some millennium balls of its own in the form of 'Naked Mideon', the first and only wrestling persona that revolved around boots, butt floss and the industry's most conveniently placed fanny pack. Fortunately for everyone, Naked Mideon's only official match was in a loss to William Regal (at the No Mercy PPV of that same year), who ironically enough would become the first member of Vince McMahon's exclusive Kiss My Ass Club just 11 months later.

When it comes to wrestling, the term 'World's Strongest Man' has been tossed around more than Jeff Hardy during a table, ladders and chairs match. In 1985 Ted Arcidi was the first man to officially bench press 700 pounds in recognised competition and soon enough he was tagged with the wrestling world's 'Strongest man' label, a tagline used solely for the big-bodied types that have less charisma

BENCH PRESSED

battle the likes of Hercules and Big John Studd, but much like his lifetime best in September 1991, when he bench pressed 725 pounds, he was unceremoniously disqualified for failing to lock his arms. Seriously, the Arcidi experiment was one that we might soon forget if not for WWE's indescribable reasoning in making an LJN Wrestling Superstar figure in his likeness. There certainly will never be another Arcidi, and while we are on the subject, failing to lock your arms during a weight lifting competition isn't that unlike forgetting to wipe your ass after dropping a massive deuce.

than a dumbbell – just ask Bill Kazmaier or Mark Henry, they will tell you. In fact, to this day, Henry is still milking the strong man gimmick even though his best work over the years was as Mae Young's 'Sexual Chocolate'.

Other than a decent showing at the WrestleMania II battle royal, and let's be honest, even NFL offensive tackle 'Jimbo' Jim Covert put up a good fight, Arcidi's WWE stint was as over as an Outback Jack promo (admit it, the 'Tie Me Kangaroo Down, Sport' chorus is still stuck in your head).

He was around long enough to

photos:Wrealanofaol.com

Unpredictable, uncooperative and out of control: these are just some of the terms that are used to describe the wild and legendary career in which Bruiser Brody helped innovate the wrestling world with his insane brawling style. The former 'Red River Jack' had a reputation for refusing to job to other wrestlers and his nomadic style of business led to many memorable trips through various wrestling promotions all over the world.

Hansen. (If you don't believe us just ask Bruno Sammartino or Rick Martel.)

In July 1988, Frank 'Bruiser Brody' Goodish was stabbed to death in a locker-room shower prior to a match with 'Dangerous' Dan Spivey while on a wrestling tour in Puerto Rico. Brody's in-ring style and his tumultuous life will never be forgotten as his memories of mayhem still live on to this day.

BRUISER BRODY
VS. THE WORLD

PhotosWrestlersWorld.com

He was perhaps the originator of what we now refer to as 'hardcore' wrestling, battling the top stars from promotion to promotion. Despite his status as a wrestling rebel of sorts, Brody was a true legend in the ring and his clashes with wrestling promoters across the globe are just as legendary as his battles inside the ropes. If blood was spilling then Brody was there, and chances are he was in the midst of one of his various feuds with the likes of Kamala, Jerry 'Crusher' Blackwell, Abdullah the Butcher, Andre the Giant and the Von Erichs.

With his wild hair and even crazier beard, Brody's brawling style earned him the reputation as a no-nonsense character that travelled around the globe in search of a good fight, even forming a tag team in Japan with fellow Gaijin bad ass Stan 'The Lariat'

There have been several incarnations of 'Team Canada' throughout the years. Similarly, many wrestlers have been dubbed or claimed to be the 'World's Strongest Man' before Mark Henry legitimately got that title. In the case of Dino Bravo, his gimmicks centred on both traits – being all muscle and a loyal Canuck.

The Italian-born and Canadian-bred Bravo (Adolfo Bresciano) wrestled on the independent circuit throughout the 1970s, competing in various territories and gaining notoriety almost instantly in single and tag team competition (he won the NWA World Tag belts with Todd Woods).

also included tagging with King Tonga – Bravo left the company, only to return with bleached blond hair a year later. The newly blond star's career took off with Luscious Johnny V. by his side. In the 'Dream Team' stable, Bravo stole some headlines from tag teammates Greg 'The Hammer' Valentine and Brutus Beefcake. Eventually, Bravo would ditch the team (not before Beefcake would first) and adopt the 'World's Strongest Man' gimmick.

Strong enough to be Sheryl Crow or anyone's man, Bravo claimed to set a world record for bench pressing at the 1988 Royal Rumble and stayed true to his

BRAVO DINO

Bravo was already beloved in his homeland when he arrived in the WWF and won the WWF World Tag Team Titles with Dominic DeNucci in the late 1970s. After a short run – which

Canadian roots by notoriously defeating All-American 'Hacksaw' Jim Duggan in a flag match at King of the Ring later that year.

In his tenure at WWF, Bravo had a few variations on his gimmick and a revolving door of managers (from Johnny V. to Frenchy Martin to Jimmy Hart), but one thing was constant: he was one strong son-uv-a-bitch. Ultimately, he'd leave the company in the early 1990s and retired altogether in 1992. A year later, he was found dead from multiple gunshots to the head. He had allegedly been murdered as a result of running an illegal cigarette smuggling business. We're not sure how he was as a man, but as a wrestler we know for sure – Bravo was a star performer.

5 SIDE SLAMMERS

★ ☆ ★ ☆ ★ ☆ ★ ☆

FIVE IMPRESSIONS WE CHALLENGE JAY LETHAL TO MASTER

1. Kamala
2. Rene Dupree
3. Paul Bearer
4. Koko B. Ware
5. Andre the Giant

Not having a gimmick was always Chris Candido's gimmick. He was a fine wrestler who left a lasting legacy thanks to the bumps he took and the impact he made in the original ECW. If only the WWE/WWF used him to their advantage.

Candido (born Candito) probably knew he was going to become a wrestler his whole life. His grandfather was 'Popeye' Chuck Richards, and a young Chris – we're guessing *sans* bleached blond hair – took to the ropes at a very young age. By the early 1990s, he had already broken into ECW with long-time girlfriend Tammy Lynn Sytch and the pair made the most of their screen time. With a look reminiscent of Dr Frank N. Furter's creation from *The Rocky Horror Picture Show*, Candido impressed right off the bat as one third of the 'Suicide Blonds' stable along with Johnny Hotbody and Chris Michaels. After a successful run in the independents, which included an NWA title, he and Sytch ended up in WWF under new 'blond' gimmicks. Candido was dubbed Skip to Tom Prichard's Zip, and Sytch, renamed Sunny, escorted the team – dubbed The Bodydonnas – to the ring. While the blonds got gold

BLOND HIGHIGHTS

(they won the WWF tag titles), it wasn't too long before Candido returned to ECW – right where he belonged. Among the many accomplishments in Paul Heyman's 'company' were capturing the tag titles with long-time foe Lance Storm, and being a part of Shane Douglas' 'Triple Threat' stable.

Fittingly, the motto for that stable was 'no gimmicks needed'. While he found success and a Cruiserweight Championship in WCW, excelled in Xtreme Pro Wrestling, and eventually returned to WWE, Candido's finest hours were always clocked in the ECW. At the time of his death in 2005, reportedly from a blood clot following post-operation surgery, he had been getting some face time on TNA Impact Wrestling. One can only wonder how many more blond highlights could've come his way.

Jim Harshman

Trained by Shawn Michaels before Y2K (or Y2J for that matter), Lance Cade showed he had a world of potential from early on. The Ohioan-born Lance McNaught was on the fast track to stardom thanks to skills he learned from the Heartbreak Kid, and caught fire after squaring off in Japan and the WWE 'minor leagues', AKA Heartland Wrestling Association. When WWE dropped HWA as a partner, Cade gained a spot at Ohio Valley Wrestling. As was the case in HWA, Cade was often paired with another potential superstar whether it was future La Resistance French flag swinger Rene Dupree or former WCW high-flyer Mark Jindrak.

Cade debuted on *Sunday Night Heat* in 2003 against Lance Storm and handily lost. He'd win the next night on *Monday Night Raw* (stealing a win while after growing somewhat stale, they'd eventually capture some of that old glory by feuding with everyone from D-Generation X to The Hardys, the latter of which they defeated to regain the tag belts.

By 2008, the Cade and Murdoch tandem lost momentum. As a result, Murdoch developed a gimmick in which he'd sing a country song, and Cade went his separate way as a dignified cowboy. The two eventually squared off against each other and Cade won. Thankfully, Murdoch eventually stopped singing.

In his last years in WWE, Cade was repackaged a few times – all a variation of his cowboy gimmick. Arguably his most memorable moment from this time was serving as sort of an enforcer

LANCE THE NIGHT AWAY

from a distracted Mr Team Canada), and soon after, began teaming with Jindrak. The two formed a formidable team, getting over as faces but eventually turning heel (working with Maven will do that to you). Their impressive run ended, however, when Jindrak was drafted to *Smackdown* the following year.

Shortly after the two separated, Cade, who had gotten heat by teaming with Jonathan Coachman (of all people), injured his knee and saw a lot of time off. By 2005, he returned to the WWE under his old name (Lance Cade), but with a new redneck gimmick alongside second-generation talent Trevor Murdoch. The pair's poor white cowboy trash gimmick worked the crowd, and within a short time, they captured the World Tag Team Championship at Unforgiven against Hurricane and Rosey. While the team broke up for a and protégé of Chris Jericho while he was feuding with HBK. Fittingly, Cade battled Michaels, and while Mr Sweet Chin Music defeated him, his career in many ways came full circle.

On October 14, 2008, Cade was released from the WWE, allegedly for drug use and an incident that took place on a plane. Realising his full potential, the company re-signed him nearly a year later after he had worked regularly on the Indy circuit but he didn't make it back to *Raw* or *Smackdown*. On August 12, 2010, Cade was found dead at his father's house from apparent heart failure brought on by mixing different drugs. He was only 29 – leaving us to wonder when he might have reached his full potential with WWE.

THE MOUNTAIN FROM STONE MOUNTAIN

Although he began his career in the 70s, Jerry Blackwell started to make a name for himself when he debuted for Verne Gagne's American Wrestling Association several years later. Battling the likes of Mad Dog Vachon, Baron Von Raschke and some guy named Hulk Hogan, the bulky but nimble star quickly earned his nickname of the 'Crusher' as he simply crushed his opponents on his way to main event status during a post-Otto Wanz AWA. In fact, years before 'Stone Cold' Steve Austin was dishing out stunners and beer baths, Blackwell was actually known as wrestling's original 'Rattlesnake'.

The Georgia native soon dropped the 'Crusher' gimmick and joined forces with Sheik Adnan Al-Kaissey. Donning full Arab regalia (almost as bad as Greg Gagne's Rambo gimmick) Blackwell captured the Tag Team Championship along with partner Ken Patera. The Sheiks would dominate the tag division for 11 months until finally dropping the gold.

In 1983 the former Sheik Ayatollah Blackwell's career reached its pinnacle when he was tapped to be the replacement for a departing good guy who was headed to WWE to spread the red and yellow love. Sadly, the Blackwell push did not have quite the same impact that the Hulkster had escaping the camel clutch as well as an eventual leg drop that would help turn wrestling into a household phenomenon.

Like 'Slaughter's Snipers' coming up short in the Team Challenge Series, Blackwell's push was mostly ill-advised and aside for a few title shots against champions Stan Hansen and Curt Hennig, the fans' favourite was eventually relegated to interview segments where he was featured driving nails into a 2x4 with his head.

Weighing up to 475 lbs, Blackwell was surprisingly quick on his feet. Among his wrestling bag of tricks was the occasional drop kick, but it was his size and strength that helped leave a big splash upon the wrestling community.

12 SIDESLAMMERS

DOZEN BEST WRESTLING PROPS

1. Mr Fuji's salt
2. Jimmy Hart's megaphone
3. Lanny Poffo's frisbee
4. The Mountie's shock stick
5. Jim Cornette's tennis racket
6. Abdullah The Butcher's fork
7. The Islanders' invisible dog leash
8. Honky Tonk Man's guitar
9. Ric Martel's Arrogance
10. Al Snow's head
11. Jim Duggan's 2 X 4
12. Brutus Beefcake's shears

THE RISE AND FALL
OF 'MADONNA'S BOYFRIEND

Making his debut at the age of 17, Louis Mucciolo Jr. began his career as a highly-respected jobber for WWE for many years as 'Louie Spicolli'. Soon working in the independents as 'Cutie Pie' and also as 'Madonna's Boyfriend' during a run with AAA as part of 'Los Gringos Locos', he then became a 'Bodydonna-in-training' as he ventured back to the WWE in 1995. This time, however, he portrayed the grunge-loving, flannel shirt-wearing 'Rad Radford' during an era that we now refer to as the Doink days of wrestling, when mean-spirited clowns (the already mentioned Doink), small clowns (Dink), sanitation workers (Duke 'The Dumpster' Droese) and evil dentists (Isaac Yankem) were given free rein to run amok on the WWE landscape (quick somebody, cue up Damien Demento's entrance music). Looking back it's no wonder the likes of HBK and Diesel 'kliq-ued' during a time that the industry was focused on making stars out of stick-wielding hockey enforcers. Speaking of which, you guys remember 'The Goon', right?

Personal issues forced the former 'Radford' to make the jump to ECW (clearly WWE saw a glimmer of potential in Mucciolo as he was released on condition that he did not work for rival WCW). In the summer of 1996 the Cali native worked a programme in the land of extreme with the 'Innovator of Violence' Tommy Dreamer. It was during this time that he began using the name 'Louie Spicolli' again as well as perfecting his neck-wrenching finisher, the 'Death Valley Driver'.

Between lingering bad habits and secret negotiations with other wrestling promotions, Spicolli left ECW under crappy terms and signed with WCW in 1997. As an associate of the New World Order, 'The Real Innovator', along with his good buddy Scott Hall and a set of stolen golf clubs, began a feud with Larry Zbyszko.

Sadly, ten years after his debut 'Spicolli' would leave behind a wrestling career that certainly had the makings of a bright future. Passing away at the age of 27 due to an overdose, the charismatic star will always be remembered for entertaining fans throughout the world as well as his innovative specialty, which in a show of respect was soon dubbed the 'Spicolli Driver'.

5 SIDESLAMMERS
FIVE STARS WHO SHOULD'VE BEEN INDUCTED INTO THE WWE HALL OF FAME BEFORE KOKO B. WARE

1. Randy Macho Man Savage
2. Jake The Snake Roberts
3. Slick
4. Rick Martel
5. Frankie

Over the years wrestling has had its fair share of WTF moments to say the least. You've seen them all before whether it be a main event storyline surrounding Kevin Federline, Shawn Michaels tag teaming with 'God' against the McMahon's, the career of Van Hammer, or of course one of our personal favourites, the Kurt Angle milk truck milk bath on the Alliance. None of these moments, however, can compare to the intimidating and unforgettable flame tattoo that spans the entire dome of Scott 'Bam Bam'

hands of sole survivor Andre the Giant. A year later a bad injury would force him to leave and require surgery to his damaged knee.

Bigelow soon resurfaced and for four years he split his wrestling travels between the NWA (National Wrestling Alliance) and NJPW (New Japan Pro Wrestling). With his immense talents, the flame-wearing big man landed back in WWE in late 1992 – first as Luna's love interest – quickly followed up as a heel member of Ted DiBiase's Million Dollar Corporation. It was around this

GREETINGS FROM ASBURY PARK

photo: Tim Harshman

Bigelow's head.

Signing with the WWE in 1987, 'the Battle for Bam Bam' soon began as the impressive big man courted the services of most managers due to his size, strength and agile ring prowess despite being close to 400 lbs. Bigelow eventually went with company newcomer 'Sir' Oliver Humperdink, which culminated in a spot on Hulk Hogan's team during the first ever Survivor Series. Despite a valiant effort, the former 'Crusher Yurkof' fell to the time that Bigelow was thrust into the national spotlight during his highly-publicised altercation with former football great Lawrence Taylor. While we can only wonder if King Kong Bundy vs. Phil McConkey was ever on the cards, Bam Bam would lose to LT but his match at WrestleMania XI helped transform him into a legit main event star and eventual 'Mania moment for years to come.

In 1997 Bigelow would bring his dominance to Philadelphia and form the Triple Threat alongside Chris Candido and 'The Franchise' Shane Douglas. Much like Thunderlips did to Rocky Balboa during the third installment of the pugilistic Hollywood adventure, Bam Bam once tossed Spike Dudley flailing into the ECW arena crowd. The Monster from Asbury Park would capture the World and Television titles during his two-year reign of pain on the 'Extreme Shah' Hack Meyers' favourite bingo hall.

In 1998 the 'Beast from the East' emerged in WCW and soon enough was thrust into the hardcore division with fellow extremists Raven and the Sandman (dare we mention Hardcore Hak). His last match in the national spotlight was on the last episode of *Nitro* against Shawn Stasiak. Bigelow departed once his contract expired after Vince McMahon and friends purchased the rights to WCW, which included a vintage library no doubt featuring the best of Sgt. Craig 'Pitbull' Pittman and yet another one of Hector Guerrero's masked mishaps, Lasertron.

In 2007, Bigelow passed away. However, his legacy remains as one of the most recognisable monsters to ever step foot in a wrestling ring thanks to his unique strength and agility for a big man. And, of course, his iconic flame tattoo.

EDDIE

He was neither the biggest nor the baddest, but Eddie Gilbert was surely one of the most entertaining characters to ever step foot in a wrestling ring. He was known throughout the industry as 'Hot Stuff' and surely he had the balls to back up his brash personality whenever he entered the arena to the sounds of the Donna Summer classic.

Beginning his storied career as most newcomers do, Gilbert's early days were filled with lots of time spent jobbing to the established stars of the WWE. Gilbert eventually traded in his losses and began to establish himself in the CWA, based out of Memphis, Tennessee. It was here that Gilbert's cocky persona started to surface most notably in his memorable feud with his former partner 'Wildfire' Tommy Rich (second to only Ronnie Garvin as the most undeserving NWA World Champion of all time).

In a time when Clara Peller was busy putting Wendy's on the map, Gilbert was building his 'Hot Stuff International Inc.' in 'Cowboy' Bill Watt's UWF (Universal Wrestling Federation). The 'Hot Stuff'-led stable of heels included both future superstars Rick Steiner and Sting as well as the always stunning Missy Hyatt. (Well, at least till 1994, anyway.)

Gilbert's greatest national exposure was wrestling for the NWA in which he teamed with former Hot Stuff Inc. cohort Steiner against Kevin Sullivan's Varsity Club, as well as a

GILBERT: UP IN FLAMES

programme against the Four Horsemen in which he helped orchestrate the triumphant return of Ricky 'The Dragon' Steamboat.

When Gilbert left WCW he also left Missy Hyatt ('Hollywood' John Tatum had to be ecstatic over that career move) and joined up with the USWA, yet another independent promotion that enabled him to book matches. In one of his final moves as an established mastermind beyond the wrestling curtain, it was Gilbert that gave up his position as head booker for the NWA's Eastern Championship Wrestling to Paul Heyman, who would eventually bring ECW to extreme new heights and help alter the landscape of wrestling forever.

Sadly Eddie Gilbert passed away at the age of 33, leaving behind a legacy that will be remembered for both his in-ring psychology as well as his behind-the-scenes genius.

photo: Wrestlanofraud.com

10 SIDESLAMMERS

TEN QUESTIONABLE PUSHES

1. Bobby Lashley
2. Steve 'Mongo' McMichael
3. Horace Hogan
4. Eugene
5. Zach Gowen
6. Scott Norton
7. Mighty Molly
8. Doink
9. Riki Rachtman Nitro Parties
10. Vampiro

Had it not been for a severe shoulder tear, Randy Poffo may have made a living catching fly balls on a baseball field instead of dropping elbows off the top rope of a wrestling ring. We've never been more thankful for an injury to have happened to someone. With baseball in his rear view, Poffo went on to become wrestling royalty. Randy 'Macho Man' Savage was a one-of-a-kind personality who battled Hulk Hogan for over a decade as the best wrestler of his time, and the biggest star with pop culture crossover appeal.

When Poffo got injured in a collision at the plate, he'd eventually have to hang up his cleats for good and put on a mask to wrestle as 'The Spider' for Gordon Sole's Florida Championship Wrestling. That gimmick eventually was dropped, and Poffo made a name for himself in various territories with his father and brother Lanny. By 1985, a star was born in the World Wrestling Federation.

From the moment Pomp and Circumstance blasted from the speakers for the first time, Savage

RANDY SAVAGE:

Poffo's path would've likely been wrestling in the first place had he not had the tools to become a successful baseball player. His father Angelo already had a strong presence in the wrestling world, and the grappling bug had probably hit his younger brother Lanny already. Still, the Ohio native debuted in the St. Louis Cardinals farm system as a teen, and went on to play minor league ball with the Cincinnati Reds and Chicago White Sox. It was during a game with the Reds that he inadvertently got his eventual wrestling nickname. When a pitch struck him, Poffo charged the pitcher and helped clear the benches. The next game, he snapped and charged the same player again, leading a newspaper reporter to question if he was trying to be a 'macho man or something.' The name would stick years later as would the term 'savage' that Ole Anderson recommended he take on.

became the most original star in sports entertainment as the 'Macho Man'. Sticking out in a crowded locker room featuring countless gimmicks, Savage caught on with his trademark G.I. Joe Monkeywrench sunglasses, shiny robe, and signature raspy voice. His manic mannerisms, mint pre-match promos (usually with Mean Gene Okerlund) and wrestling prowess instantly popped the crowd, and with Miss Elizabeth escorting him to the ring, pre-pubescent teens in the audience probably felt the first pop in their pants.

In his first year with the WWF, Savage feuded with many, but notably with Tito Santana, who he'd eventually defeat for the Intercontinental Championship in 1986 – the year, incidentally, his former Cardinals teammate Keith Hernandez and the Mets would win the World Series. That year was pretty big for Savage as well. He feuded with

George Steele for the better part of the year because he was crushing on Liz. At WrestleMania II Savage beat 'The Animal', but their history together continued at WrestleMania III. While Hulk Hogan versus Andre the Giant was marketed as the main event, and it sort of lived up to that hype, the bout everyone was talking about the next morning (and still do today) was Savage against Ricky Steamboat. Both stars were notoriously known throughout the industry as the best in the business and they clearly didn't disappoint. In

Championship at WrestleMania IV.

Savage held the belt for over a year, while the Mega Powers continued to dominate tag action. By 1989, however, Savage had had enough of the Hulkster moving in on his valet. Fearing he wanted Elizabeth all for himself, the two megastars feuded for years. Savage dropped the belt to Hogan at WrestleMania V, and teamed with Zeus to fight his *No Holds Barred* co-star Hogan and Brutus Beefcake at SummerSlam.

OH YEAHWWWWW

an epic battle that saw 19 two-counts, 'The Dragon' ultimately beat the 'Macho Man' thanks to interference by old nemesis Steele.

For the rest of the 1980s, Savage and Hogan were viewed as the two faces of the company. As mentioned, their appeal extended far beyond a wrestling ring with Hogan garnering the *Sports Illustrated* cover and making terrible movies and Savage becoming spokesman for Slim Jim… 'oh yeaaaaaaaaah!' In the ring, the two dominated, forming the Mega Powers. The two were big in singles competition as well with Savage winning the King of the Ring tournament in 1987 and a 14-man tournament for the WWF

Savage, who traded in Miss Elizabeth for Sensational Sherri that year, would go on to adopt the 'Macho King' name after winning the King of the Ring title from Jim Duggan. While he took on his fair share of opponents, he still feuded with Hogan. By 1990, however, he shifted his attention to then-champion the Ultimate Warrior. While he never beat the Warrior for the belt, he did cost Warrior the title against Sgt. Slaughter the next year.

Eventually, Warrior and Savage's feud came to a head with a career-on-the-line match at WrestleMania VII, which the Macho King lost. For the next few months, with Miss Elizabeth back in the fray after Sherri had turned on him following his 'Mania loss, Savage served as a colour commentator. In one of the finest moments in WWF history, Savage proposed and went on to marry his then-real-life wife Elizabeth at SummerSlam in 1991. Eventually, Savage would be reinstated by fake president Jack Tunney, and took to the ring against the likes of Jake 'The Snake' Roberts and Ric Flair. Speaking of the 'Nature Boy', Savage beat him for his second World Championship at WrestleMania VIII.

Once Savage dropped the belt to Flair, he tag teamed with Ultimate Warrior to become the 'Ultimate Maniacs'. That tandem didn't last long, and Savage was soon calling more matches than he was actually wrestling in. In a somewhat surprising move in October 1994, Savage let his WWF contract run out and signed with their main competitor, WCW.

When he arrived in Ted Turner land, Savage found himself feuding with some familiar faces like Flair and Hogan. As was the case in the WWF, Savage found a high level of success in WCW, winning their championship belt four times. He also reunited with Miss Elizabeth. Aside from the girl and the gold, Savage had many key moments in the company. For starters, he was involved in the best storyline we've ever seen. At Bash at the Beach it was he who Hulk Hogan turned his back on (as well as Sting and Lex Luger) to form the nWo with Scott Hall and Kevin Nash. Eventually, Savage would become an integral part in the original nWo and Nash's 'Wolfpac' spin-off.

While he took part in WCW as it started to sink (you remember the slicked-back ponytail and Gorgeous George, right?), Savage's screen time lessened more and more. By the time Vince McMahon purchased WCW, the Macho Man was long gone. In 2002, he resurfaced – not in the ring, but on film as Spider-Man's nemesis in the wrestling ring – Bonesaw McGraw. For years after that, he did voice roles in a few films, and released an ill-fated rap album. By 2004, he was back where he belonged – the ring. While his time in TNA Wrestling was far from memorable, he got over.

On May 10, 2010, he married long-time girlfriend Barbara Lynn Payne, and sadly a year later (May 20 to be exact) he suffered a fatal heart attack, aged 58, while driving with his wife in Florida. To try to capture Savage's impact and legacy in a brief segment within a wrestling book featuring other stars is a somewhat impossible feat. Savage paved the way for so many heels and multi-dimensional wrestling stars who beat to their own drum.

The action of current star CM Punk on the first *Monday Night Raw* following his death says it all. That night Punk wore Savage's trademark 'star' trunks. Clearly Punk knew that without Savage, there would be no Punk. So many wrestlers probably feel that way. So many fans miss him, respect him, and wish he was still dropping patented elbows from the top turnbuckle.

Whether she was scary or sensuous there is no denying that Sherri Martel was indeed wrestling royalty. In a world occupied by the likes of pre-Diva Divas the Glamour Girls, the Jumping Bomb Angels, Velvet McIntyre, Debbie Combs and Rockin' Robin, not to mention the 27-year title reign of the Fabulous Moolah, Sensational Sherri managed to stand tall above the best and baddest ladies the WWE had to offer.

Like most greats, Martel eventually made her way to the WWE, debuting in the summer of 1987 and quickly defeating the Fabulous Moolah for the Women's Championship. Her sensational reign lasted for 15 months until dropping the gold to Rockin' Robin. Phasing out the women's division much like they phased out midget wrestling at that time as well as current-day tag team wrestling, Sherri turned her attention once again to being a manager.

SHERRI MARTEL

LONG LIVE THE QUEEN OF WRESTLING

Her groundbreaking career began in 1985, debuting in the AWA and capturing the company's World Women's Championship from Candi Devine at SuperClash, a co-promotional event held by the AWA and NWA in order to combat the WWE's advancing world takeover. Martel was a gifted talent whose three-time reign as AWA champion put her in the upper echelon of all-time women wrestlers, channelling past greats such as Mildred Burke, Vivian Vachon and Penny Banner.

Aside from her in-ring dominance Martel was also a masterful manager, guiding the improbable team of 'Playboy' Buddy Rose and 'Pretty Boy' Doug Somers to the tag team mountaintop and an 'ESPN Classic' feud with Marty Jannetty and Shawn Michaels (more on this mullet-haired boy toy a little later).

It was here that the future Hall of Famer found her greatest success smack dab in the middle of such classic feuds as Hulk Hogan and Brutus Beefcake vs. Randy Savage and Zeus, as well as her legendary cat fights with Elizabeth and Sapphire. When Savage was crowned King after defeating 'Hacksaw' Jim Duggan, Martel was rightfully crowned 'Queen', eventually relinquishing her crown after the 'Macho King' lost a career match to Parts Unknown's favourite son, the Ultimate Warrior.

In between short managing stints with 'Million Dollar Man' Ted DiBiase and Tatanka respectively, the loud-mouthed vixen helped usher in the historic singles career of the 'Heartbreak Kid' Shawn Michaels, even singing his obnoxious entrance theme 'Sexy Boy'.

In 1994 Sensuous Sherri emerged in WCW where she worked a programme as manager of the 'Nature Boy' Ric Flair. Her next venture, and perhaps her most rewarding, was as Sister Sherri, leader of the seven-time WCW Tag Team Champions Harlem Heat consisting of Booker T and his often-forgotten older bro Stevie Ray (slapjack, anyone).

Whether she was inside the ring or out, Sherri Martel was in a class all of her own. Passing away in 2007, the Queen of the ring will always be remembered as one of women's wrestling's greatest ambassadors.

10 SIDE SLAMMERS

TEN BEST OR HALFWAY DECENT SPORTS STAR CAMEOS IN WRESTLING

1. Pete Rose, WrestleMania
2. Mike Tyson, WrestleMania XIV
3. Billy Martin, WrestleMania I
4. Lawrence Taylor, WrestleMania XVI
5. Dennis Rodman, WCW
6. William 'The Fridge' Perry, WrestleMania II
7. Dick Butkis, WrestleMania II
8. Bob Ueker, WrestleMania III, IV
9. Karl Malone, WCW
10. Buster Douglas, SNME

What Evel Knievel was to death-defying stunts Mike Shaw was to wrestling gimmicks that never had a snowball's chance in hell. Before his brush with fame in the greener pastures of WCW and WWE, Shaw wrestled in 1982 for Stu Hart's Stampede Wrestling in Calgary, Alberta, Canada under the guise of Makhan Singh.

With just as much credibility as the rapping wrestler P.N. News, Shaw's of the cloth who despite his penchant for inflicting pain upon opponents also looked like he had no issue finding his way around a Chinese buffet. However, Shaw's monkish gimmick was not very well received among certain members of the Catholic Church and soon enough wrestling's first and only dancing priest was gone.

Grotesque is the best way to describe Shaw's last but most popular persona,

REMEMBERING
NORMAN THE LUNATIC

foray into World Championship Wrestling was in the form of a 400-pound madman by the name of Norman the Lunatic. With his medical scrubs and Bruiser Brody-esque facial fury, Norman's not-so-dramatic impact on the industry indeed ranks up there with the very best of Brakkus.

Soon, however, Shaw traded in his 'straight outta the Asylum' gimmick for a much more fan-friendly persona. No doubt the wrestling world was never quite ready for Trucker Norm, and just like that, the Michigan resident was headed to the WWE to embark on a series of forgettable characters that were better suited to a carnival freak show than a wrestling ring.

In spring 1993 the world was introduced to 'Friar Ferguson', a man 'Bastion Booger'. In a monumental time when WWE simply had no idea how to make stars, Shaw was repackaged in 1994 as the repulsive and disgusting Booger, that like most bad farts, still lingers to this very day. At the end of 2007, after years away from the spotlight, Booger was picked to be a part of the 15th anniversary of *Monday Night Raw*. Just three years later Shaw passed away at the age of 53 from a heart attack.

Whether he was jobbing to WCW stars as the insane Norman or simply grossing us all out as the highly inappropriate germ of wrestling, Mike Shaw certainly left his mark on the industry – although it was not a very pretty one.

Long before Jack Palance made one-handed push-ups fashionable at the Oscars, 'Playboy' Buddy Rose was doing them justice on 'Piper's Pit' and in various wrestling rings. Like the Oscar-winning City Slicker, there was more to Rose than getting down on all fours.

Born Paul Perschman, Rose studied wrestling under the tutelage of legend Verne Gagne in the early 1970s. Throughout that groovy decade, he

athletic opponents and challenging Bob Backlund for the heavyweight title.

After leaving the WWF for many years, he eventually returned for WrestleMania as the masked Executioner and continued to generate cheap heat with his heavy-heeled gimmick. By the 1990s, he retired from the business to open a wrestling training school. The master of the Las Vegas Jackpot still dabbled in the ring

EVERY ROSE HAS ITS THORN

wrestled in the AWA, Pacific Northwest Wrestling and the WWF, feuding with the likes of a pre-Sgt. Slaughter Sgt. Slaughter and Jimmy 'Superfly' Snuka. In the early 1980s he became one of the top heels for the WWF, escorted to the ring by the Grand Wizard, and getting heat for his ego (only Rose could pull off a fat-guy-thinking-he's-in-shape gimmick). During this span, Rose made his mark by taking on more

through the years. On April 28, 2009, Rose was found dead, allegedly due to complications from his weight and diabetes. A star that often flies under the radar, Rose was as big a star as anyone in the AWA (winning multiple championships), as well as the NWA, and held his own with everyone from Roddy Piper to Bobby Heenan in the WWF.

10 SIDESLAMMERS

HOME SWEET HOME:
WRESTLING'S MOST CREATIVE RESIDENCES

1. Death Valley – Undertaker
2. Anywhere He Damn Well Pleases – Sid Vicious
3. An Undisclosed Location – Eric Young
4. Parts Unknown – Ultimate Warrior
5. The Future – The New Breed
6. Truth or Consequences, New Mexico – Cactus Jack
7. 20,000 Leagues Under The Sea – Shark Boy
8. Bombay, Michigan – Sabu
9. Badstreet, USA – Fabulous Freebirds
10. The Last House On The Left – Hack Myers

COWBOY
UP!

From *The Lone Ranger* to *Brokeback Mountain*, cowboys have had a long-standing history of success in pop culture. The same can be said for the world of wrestling, which has seen its fair share of wranglers thrive from Terry Funk to Outlaw Ron Bass. Bobby Duncum Jr. was a young buckaroo that showed a world of promise when he debuted with a similar gimmick in the early 1990s.

The Texan started wrestling independently before debuting in All Japan Pro Wrestling and thriving in singles and tag matches. While he was trying to make a name for himself overseas, Duncum continued to wrestle in the States, eventually landing in Extreme Championship Wrestling (ECW) by 1997. He actually wrestled for both AJPW and ECW at the same time before joining World Championship Wrestling (WCW) in 1998. The rising star began his WCW career feuding with Chris Jericho but failing to gain his TV title. Eventually, he'd form a face tag team with Mike Enos before ditching that for a heel turn.

With the stable West Texas Rednecks, Duncum really found his identity. Joined by legend Curt Hennig and Barry and Kendall Windham, the stable took part in many memorable matches and feuds, notably with the No Limit Soldiers, before disbanding after failing to capture any gold.

On January 24, 2000, Duncum died of an apparent accidental overdose of painkillers, which he had taken following rotator cuff surgery. He was just 34. A versatile wrestler with a gimmick that worked just as well for him as it did his dad, we can only speculate where his career would've gone in a post-WCW world.

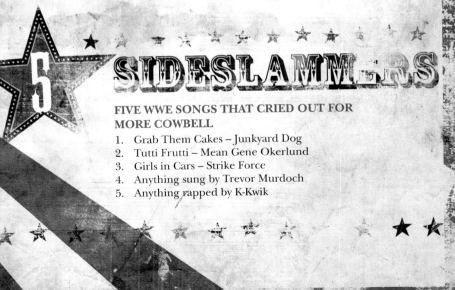

5 SIDESLAMMERS

FIVE WWE SONGS THAT CRIED OUT FOR MORE COWBELL

1. Grab Them Cakes – Junkyard Dog
2. Tutti Frutti – Mean Gene Okerlund
3. Girls in Cars – Strike Force
4. Anything sung by Trevor Murdoch
5. Anything rapped by K-Kwik

Any child of the 1980s grew up listening to (and watching) the classic banter between colour commentators Gorilla Monsoon, Jesse 'The Body' Ventura and Bobby 'The Brain' Heenan. To put it simply, no one was better at calling a match than those three announcing greats. That said, long before he donned a suit and ring professionally. Originally known as light-hearted Italian Gino Marella (yes, current scene-stealer Santino Marella was named after him), he eventually turned heel as the grizzly Gorilla Monsoon from Manchuria, a man essentially raised by bears. With his new gimmick, he sparkled for Vince McMahon Sr. in the 1960s, became a

GORILLA
IN OUR MIDST

sat next to a future Minnesota governor and a weasel, Monsoon (born Robert Marella) was an intimidating presence inside the ring.

Built like a dump truck, Marella was a sports star and accomplished amateur wrestler in high school and college. His collegial skills caught the eye of the wrestling world and it wasn't too long before he found himself in the

star for his new friend's company, and even became a shareholder.

In the WWWF (later WWF and even later WWE), Monsoon feuded with another fun-loving Italian, Bruno Sammartino. Eventually, Monsoon competed in tag competitions, winning the Tag Team Championship with fellow future WWE Hall of Famer Killer Kowalski. By 1969, Monsoon turned face and arguably became a bigger star – especially in his native New York City. By the early 1980s, his career was coming to an end. After losing a career-on-the-line match again Ken Patera, he hung up his boots for good – although he competed on rare occasions.

As we all know by now, Monsoon became a staple in the announcing booth with Jesse 'The Body' Ventura and eventually Heenan. Just as he had forged a friendship and helped add oomph to storylines backstage for Vince Sr., Monsoon befriended Vince McMahon Jr., who moved him from the ring to the announcer's chair.

In so many ways, Monsoon was the voice of the WWF. He called the first eight WrestleManias and broke down matches on various weekly programming. He also notably took part in hilarious vignettes with Heenan – always playing the straight man to 'The Brain's' antics.

Marella stepped down as the WWF's lead announcer at WrestleMania IX, and was replaced by Jim Ross – another icon in the business. From time to time, much as he had done lacing his boots, Monsoon would return to the mic and called matches on several occasions. While he wasn't a force on TV as he had been, Monsoon continued to help develop the federation behind the scenes. By 1995 he was named president of the company, replacing former fake president Jack

Tunney. Health problems relating to his diabetes restricted Monsoon's involvement with the company shortly thereafter. His last TV appearance was at WrestleMania XV, where he served as a judge in a contest involving Butterbean and Bart Gunn. That match was so very unmemorable but provided the crowd with an opportunity to cheer their beloved legend on in full force for all that he brought to the table.

On October 6, 1999, Gorilla Monsoon passed away from heart failure as a result of diabetes at just 62 years old. His voice and legacy live on.

Although his 'Brawl for All' performance stands alongside WCW's Ultimate Warrior doppelganger The Renegade as one of the game's biggest disappointments, Steve Williams by far is one of the toughest MF'ers to ever set foot in a wrestling ring. Dubbed 'Dr Death' dating back to his junior high days, the wrestling legend was also a collegiate All-American out of the University of Oklahoma.

The Oklahoma Stampede first powered on to the scene in 1986 as part of the Universal Wrestling Federation, the same fed that helped usher in the careers of the Ultimate Warrior and Sting, who were then known as Blade Runner Rock and Flash. The college standout and PWI cover-boy who went on to capture the UWF Heavyweight title from a pre-Guardian Angel Big Bubba Rogers was soon given a push in the NWA after Crockett Promotions bought the smaller-market company in late 1987.

His NWA accolades, which include a role in the Varsity Club, culminated in both a United States Tag Team Championship with Kevin Sullivan and a World Tag Team Championship with Mike Rotunda. The Club soon went its separate ways and soon Williams became the biggest and baddest Japanese import since Godzilla.

As part of All Japan Pro Wrestling, 'Dr Death' formed an unstoppable tag team with former Freebird Terry Gordy and in the process he also quickly became a main event star in the land of the rising sun. For over a decade Williams dominated the Far East wrestling scene until his ill-fated arrival back on US soil to take part in the WWE's 'Brawl for All' competition. The legit fighting tournament was supposed to be Dr Death's big break but thanks to a solid Bart Gunn punch Williams' push and probably his mystique upon the Japanese population plummeted.

There is no doubt that Dr Death was as bad as they came and his courageous battle against throat cancer in 2004 was a testament to his legit toughness both in and out of the ring. Sadly his fight ended five years later in 2009. However, Steve Williams will forever remain as one of the top foreign competitors in Japanese wrestling history.

DOCTOR DEATH

In the 1980s, following years of having to watch a major wrestling event at your local arena, showing it closed-circuit, pay-per-view (PPV) came to our households and we all revelled in how we could watch the Superbowl of wrestling (AKA WrestleMania) in the comfort of our own home. As more time went by, additional wrestling events were added like the Thanksgiving feast known as Survivor Series, the mid-winter classic the Royal Rumble, and the August summer swansong called SummerSlam.

Each of these events felt like mini-Superbowls for the wrestling world. We'd buy chips, dips, and if we were over 21, a couple of six-packs to cheer our heroes and heels on. But, something happened in the mid-to-late 1990s that spoiled the party. For starters, WCW became viable competitors to WWF, and started holding their own must-buy PPVs. Then ECW started gaining traction and served as a viable alternative for both companies. Then WWF started holding their PPVs monthly, and the rest followed suit. Nowadays, there's only one viable company in WWE (sorry kids, TNA or Impact Wrestling doesn't count), but they continue to have PPVs once a month. We long for the days when pay-per-view events were once or up to four times a year. The monthly moneymakers have lessened the power of events like the core four (WrestleMania, Royal Rumble, SummerSlam and Survivor Series) and have made our wallets smaller than they really need to be. Who thought of this concept, Irwin R. Schyster?

WHAT...
ARE WE MADE OF MONEY?

10 SIDESLAMMERS

TOP TEN LJN FIGURES THAT WERE NEVER MADE

1. Brother Love
2. Rene Goulet
3. Lord Alfred Hayes
4. Lelani Kai
5. Sgt. Slaughter
6. Howard Finkel
7. Cousin Luke
8. Paul Roma
9. 'The Natural' Butch Reed
10. Jacques Rougeau

For a man dubbed 'the bulldog', Davey Boy Smith was more like a cat in that he had nine lives. The wrestling giant overcame many personal issues such as addiction and injuries, and to a lesser degree bad dreadlocks and a four-legged mascot, to put together a career that quite easily is one of the finest in wrestling history. That's saying quite a lot when you factor in that he passed away at just 39.

Wrestling was clearly in Smith's blood from the womb on out. Whereas most 15-year-olds get off by playing videogames or collecting baseball cards, 'Young Davey' was establishing himself in the wrestling ring, competing professionally on TV show *World of Sport* in his native UK. The Manchester native wrestled there for several years before catching the eye of the infamous Hart family.

A Padawan to wrestling Jedi Stu Hart, Smith honed his skills in Calgary, learning the ropes at the infamous Dungeon. Often working opposite cousin and future tag team partner Tom Billington, AKA Dynamite Kid, Smith excelled in Hart's Stampede Wrestling, and grew even closer to the family when he married Stu Hart's daughter Diana in 1984.

Before landing in the WWF, Smith gained traction by simultaneously wrestling with Stampede as well as New Japan Pro Wrestling, where he and the Dynamite Kid ended their 'feud'. After a brief stint as the British Bulldogs in All Japan Pro Wrestling, Smith and Billington joined the WWF and quickly made us forget about other British export Giant Haystacks. In a solid first year, the tandem quickly became fans' favourites, feuding with fellow newcomers (and family members) the Hart Foundation (Bret Hart and Jim Neidhart) as well as the Dream Team of Greg 'The Hammer' Valentine and Brutus Beefcake.

At WrestleMania II the Bulldogs, who were led by Capt. Lou Albano, beat the Dream Team to take the Tag Team Championship titles. During a run that lasted throughout most of the year, the Bulldogs successfully defended their belts against a bevy of tag team royalty that included 'Goonies R Good Enuff' music video icons Nikolai Volkoff and the Iron Sheik. For several years,

DAVEY WAS A GOLIATH

the Bulldogs appeared regularly in wrestling programming, and never lost momentum – even when they were given a mascot named Matilda. Backstage heat – mostly on the Dynamite Kid – led them to leave the WWF but that wasn't the last we'd hear of Smith and the WWF. While the pair continued to wrestle as a team briefly outside of the WWF universe, they would eventually split up, and Smith returned to the WWF as a singles competitor.

Slightly repackaged as the 'British Bulldog', a dreadlocked Smith ran wild in the WWF, capturing the Intercontinental title in an epic match against his brother-in-law Bret Hart at SummerSlam 1992 at Wembley Stadium in London. Smith's return was short-lived, however, when he was released along with the Ultimate Warrior for reportedly receiving human growth hormones (HGH).

After a short stint in the WCW (he was released following an apparent bar fight), Smith made his return to the WWF in 1994, keeping it 'in the family' by teaming with Bret Hart against Owen Hart and Jim Neidhart. After teaming with Lex Luger briefly as one half of the Allied Powers, Smith turned heel and feuded with Diesel for quite a while. He also challenged Bret Hart and later Shawn Michaels for the WWF Championship title but came up short.

After many successes in the WWF, including a victory over Owen Hart to claim the then-newly-created European Championship, as well as being part of a new Hart Foundation stable, Smith left for WCW in 1997 with Neidhart. His stay in the Ted Turner company was brief. After a string of injuries sidelined him, he was cut loose from the company. This paved the way for yet another return to where he belonged all along.

In September 1999, Smith returned to the WWF for the final time. Trading in his usual ring garb, Smith appeared more rugged, wrestling in jeans and going hardcore. Speaking of which, he'd take home the Hardcore title, regain the European Championship, and feud with The Rock in this run. The latter battle famously ended with him being thrown in some dung in an 'Attitude' era match.

Behind the scenes, Smith allegedly had a problem with pain medication and other drugs. In 2000, he checked into rehab and was released by the WWF shortly thereafter. He died on May 18, 2002 from a heart attack, allegedly from past steroid use and HGH. While he never won the WWF Heavyweight Championship and had many ups and downs in his career, by all accounts, Davey Boy Smith was a true champion in the industry. He was a man who gave so much to wrestling, and had so much more to give.

THE POSSE IS IN EFFECT

For all the various New World Order and Four Horsemen incarnations over the years there has been just one heel-influenced faction that has stayed true to its villainous core.

In 1999 WWE introduced the Mean Street Posse, a group led by Shane McMahon, which included his childhood pals Pete Gas and Rodney as well as sort-of-established pro wrestler Joey Abs.

With sweater vests and khaki pants in tow, the Posse, who hailed from the mean streets of Greenwich, Connecticut, were first introduced to do Shane's dirty work and eventually became the tag team equivalent of a human punching bag, taking bumps and bruises from most of the top teams in the WWE at the time.

As Pearl Shay once ruled the roost over her '227' neighbours, so have the Mean Street Posse in regards to the well-off patrons of Greenwich Avenue. Their career highlight was at WrestleMania 2000 when all three Posse members briefly held the WWE Hardcore title. Although they disbanded after only a year together in the spotlight, one thing is for certain – the Mean Street Posse brought instant 'street cred' to the world of wrestling despite always competing in argyle sweaters.

YES VIRGINIA THERE WAS A XANTA CLAUS

Before he became everyone's favourite hardcore chair-swinging freak in tune with the extreme masses that chanted 'Balls!' every time he smashed an opponent with a swift kick or punch, John Rechner's path to wrestling superstardom made a brief and almost forgettable stop with WWE in 1995.

The Nutley, New Jersey star, whose wrestling résumé includes an appearance on the holiday-inspired 'Massacre on 34th Street' ECW pay-per-view in December 2000, was also a devious part of WWE's 'In Your House: Seasons Beatings' event, when he appeared as the very Grinch-y Xanta Claus. Rechner, whose best work in the ring would be as fans' favourite Balls Mahoney, was brought in by Ted

DiBiase as Santa's evil twin brother. Hailing from the South Pole and hell-bent on stealing presents as opposed to giving them, the evil St Nick gimmick was once again proof that in the world of wrestling 'everyone has a price' – even jolly old Santa Claus.

Thankfully for children everywhere Xanta's holiday exploits lasted just as long as a Cabbage Patch Doll did on shelves during Black Friday in 1984. Rechner was clearly on the 'naughty' list until he started entering the ring to AC/DC's 'Big Balls' and started dropping friend and foe alike on to flaming tables, a move which ironically, in the land of extreme, will get you quickly back on to the 'nice' list.

They were Conquerors of the world but when it came to wrestling they will go down as a team best known for enhancing more fortunate talent on their way to the top of the ladder. In full golden spandex from head to toe, the masked men billed from 'somewhere in Latin America' burst on to the WWE scene in 1987. Clashing with some of wrestling's most celebrated tag teams like The Killer Bees, The Rockers and The Fabulous

photo:Wrealano@aol.com

LOS CONQUISTADORS

Rougeau Brothers, the mystery grapplers (actually unmasked mid-carders Jose Luis Rivera and Jose Estrada) always seemed to put up a good fight but almost surely seemed to be on the losing end.

Although their unsuccessful track record made them more or less the 'Iron' Mike Sharpe of tag team wrestling, the golden hombres actually fared quite well in their first and only pay-per-view appearance at the inaugural Survivor Series in November 1988. Despite yet another appearance in the loss column, they remained in the 10-team elimination all the way to the very end before being knocked

off by Legion of Doom leftovers the Powers of Pain.

Years later the golden bodysuits re-emerged as the Conquistadors and made several brief appearances during WWE programming as recently as the early 2000s during the height of the Tables, Ladders and Chairs wars in which the roles of 'Uno' and 'Dos' were portrayed by Edge and Christian as well as the Hardy Boys.

Despite conquering nothing in the ring, the golden boys, who sparkled brighter than a Dustin Rhodes unitard or a pair of vintage AWA Bockwinkel trunks, almost always finished last but remain numero uno in our wrestling loving hearts.

12 SIDESLAMMERS

TWELVE FAMOUS AND NOT SO FAMOUS WRESTLING BROTHERS

1. The Rougeau Brothers
2. Brother Bruti
3. Kevin and Evad Sullivan
4. The Smokin' Gunns
5. The Hardy Boyz
6. The Highlanders
7. The Von Erichs
8. The Godwinns
9. The Funks
10. Bret and Owen Hart
11. Chad and James Dick
12. The Brisco Brothers

THE MODERN DAY WARRIOR

World Class Championship Wrestling was the breeding ground for some of the most influential stars in the history of the business. For example, before he was rambling nonsense and dominating the WWE as the Ultimate Warrior, Jim Hellwig was earning his stripes in Texas as the Dingo Warrior. Let's not forget 'Gentleman' Chris Adams' star pupil Steve Austin, who was stunningly impressive during his debut at the Dallas Sportatorium years before he was dropping F-bombs upon the wrestling universe.

Which brings us to one of the best-known families in wrestling history, the Von Erich family (minus pseudo cousin Lance), comprised of a rich history of squared circle royalty led by family patriarch Fritz Von Erich.

Taking the wrestling world by storm (hence his future WWE nickname 'The Texas Tornado'), Kerry Von Erich was perhaps the most well-known and successful member of the entire Von Erich clan. In the spring of 1984 the 'Modern Day Warrior' reached the highlight of his career by defeating Ric Flair at Texas Stadium during the highly emotional 'David Von Erich

Parade of Champions'. Although his reign lasted only 18 days the World Class Warrior soon set his sights on memorable moments against the likes of the Fabulous Freebirds, Gino Hernandez and Jerry 'The King' Lawler.

In the summer of 1990 Von Erich made his debut for WWE on *Saturday Night's Main Event*. His brief but memorable whirlwind through the federation that once introduced us to Brock Lesnar, Battle Cat and Man Mountain Rock, was highlighted by an Intercontinental Championship title run along with a WrestleMania VII victory against Dino Bravo.

Just as infamous as the Von Erich claw was the family's penchant for tragedy. In February 1993 Kerry Von Erich took his life amidst his constant struggle with substance abuse over the years. In 2009 the entire Von Erich family was posthumously inducted into the WWE's Hall of Fame, solidifying a permanent place shared with other wrestling immortals and a spot amongst the battle royal in the sky's greatest gods.

Superfly JIMMY SNUKA
WRESTLER RUN-IN

'I was a cliff diver back in the islands. I still dive off cliffs. If ones are around, I'll go off it anyway. That's how it all started. When I got into the business, I started off in Portland, Oregon and all the places around there. It was really sweet.

'I love going out there and entertaining the fans. My whole spirit is there. I look forward to walking in the ring, hearing the fans cheer and turn me on, and then I turn them on, brother. I always liked to give the fans something different every time. I'm always wearing a different outfit. I love it, bro. It's just like turning the pages of a book, and it gets exciting. That's what I like to do for the fans.'

SPECIAL THANKS FROM THE AUTHORS

Jon Chattman would like to thank his wife Alison for her love and support, and for putting up with all of his extracurricular writing gigs that sadly pay him only in fulfillment. He'd like to thank his rock star newborn son Noah for being the best thing he's ever created – poopy diapers and all.

He'd like to thank his tag team partner Rich Tarantino for coming up with this book's concept (after careful planning), and for being one of his closest friends ever since Hulk Hogan turned heel with the nWo. Without Rich, there is no *Battle Royal* book. That said, he's still waiting for my EEW royalties. Jon would like to thank Paul and Jane with Pitch for publishing this book, Dean for editing it, and Duncan for putting it all together. Thanks to Mike Lano for providing this book with many amazing shots. Thanks also to Tim Harshman, Peter Lederberg, Tim Hornbaker, Andy Vineberg and Bobby Begun. Thanks to Al Snow for his Patrick Duffy-laden kick ass foreword, and to all the wonderful wrestlers who contributed to this book especially Shane Helms. He wishes to also thank his parents for their endless support – specifically his dad for taking him to all of those wrestling shows as a kid, and picking up all those wrestling figures (Masters and Toy and Sports Warehouse) along the way to the show.

He especially thanks John Miele for his endless support, his Andre the Giant Bear acquisition and above all else, his sorely-needed fountain of wrestling knowledge. Thanks to Brew Crewer Allie Tarantino for Swedish Fish nights and Yogisms for that other book and always being in Rich and my corner.

Chattman also thanks the following people for their assistance in friendship, inspiration, and/or support throughout the years (some are gone but not forgotten): Alyson Tina, Keith Troy, The Luxemburgs, James Mullally, Andrew Plotkin, Dante Mercadante, Seymour Spoons, Shira Tarantino, Carol Nordgren, Larry Harbison, Billy Ray Briley, and Carol Shiffman.

This book is dedicated to Randy Savage, a man who lived up to the hype I built up in my head for decades. Chattman would also like to dedicate this to his best friend Stephen Spruck, who got him back into watching wrestling at the height of the Monday Night Wars. Without Steve, he would've been content having watched his last match in The Ultimate Warrior reign. Miss and love you, Steve. Your memory lives on in Noah.

Rich Tarantino would like to thank his amazing wife Erica for her support, love and for dealing with my passion for everything headlocks, heel turns and Hogan foam fingers. Thanks to my son Jaxon who I can't wait to share my obsession for wrestling with.

Thanks to my tag partner Jon Chattman. From the Sweet 'Stache to Fenway you truly are the Jacques to my Ray Rougeau… thanks and 'nice boots' brother.

Thanks to Allie Tarantino for buying 17 copies of this book despite access to the 'Missing Link' group. Thanks bro for putting me over all these years… keep on staganatin' !!!

To my parents, Ralph and Diane Tarantino. Mom, thanks for showing the love for my favourite soap opera not called *Days of Our Lives* and Dad, thanks for tracking down my figures and for letting 'The Beast' leap off the top bunk…

Thanks to the Real John Miele, muchas gracias Senor Miele! Viva Bigote!

Thanks to Joe and Rachel Amori. Joe, 12-hour mania marathons and watching the return of Hulkamania from our seats in heaven, damn I miss those black box PPVs on 7th street! Rachel, hope this book finds its way into your little girl's library and she has the same passion for wrestling as you do, thank you both for your support and friendship and for allowing El Feardoe to crash your special day.

Thanks to Chip the Bruiser Barone, glad we finally got to mix it up and settle our feud once and for all.

Thanks to Anthony DeCicco for your friendship and rivalled admiration for a Sycho Sid promo. Now get me those damn plates and most importantly find that damn list!

I would also like to extend a special thank you to all of the following: Pitch Publishing, El Feardoe, Mr Domerica, The Puma, Mama Agostino, EEW, SSD, and the Prince's Clown.

Finally, thanks to 'The Animal' George Marcin for our countless wrestling adventures and for dubbing me with the 'Little Richie Ding Dong' persona.

This book is dedicated to the memory of Brian Pillman and Lionel Giroux.

photo:Wrealargo@aol.com

Superfly
JIMMY SNUKA
WRESTLER RUN-IN

On inspirations:
'André the Giant. When I met that brother, we just clicked. We became really good friends.'

On deaths:
'I've loved them all, man. I loved every one of them. I love this whole world.'

On mic skills vs. wrestling:
'I'd rather wrestle. That's my whole life and spirit. I love what I do. I enjoy it. I love going out there and entertaining fans. My whole spirit is there. I look forward to walking in the ring, hearing them cheer – that turns me on, and they know I'm going to turn them on.'

On watching:
'I still watch it. I watch all these young kids. I get to do these autograph sessions, and I get to meet them. That's really nice.'

On advice:
'Do the right thing and everything will be OK after that. When you love something, you can't go halfway. You have to go all the way.'

On other wrestlers:
'There are a lot of great characters. We encourage each other and learn from each other from communicating. You have to protect the body. Nobody is number one. We go in the ring and it's not to get hurt. It's to support our family.'

On wrestling now:
'I still wrestle independents. I'm still flying around. When I go to people in the locker room after, people ask, "how was he?" They say, "brother, you don't even feel him."'

photo: Bobby Begun

ABOUT THE AUTHORS

Jon Chattman once ate a Reuben sandwich with 'Macho Man' Randy Savage and asked Triple H if his children ever spewed out formula (much like he does with water before entering the ring) after playing a 'game' of Chutes and Ladders. These are just two career highlights from the lifelong wrestling fan and professional writer.

Through a career of over 15 years, Jon Chattman body slammed the written word (whatever that means) for a variety of outlets including the *New York Post*, *Wizard*, and Spinner.com. For over five years, Chattman has owned and operated thecheappop.com, a pop culture humour site that specialises in down-to-earth celebrity interviews, music and entertainment reviews. His blog posts for the site have appeared regularly on the *Huffington Post* since 2008.

In 2011, he created an intimate musical series site called asidesmusic.com.

In May 2009, he co-authored *Sweet 'Stache*, a humour book on celebrity mustaches, with Rich Tarantino. The book and authors were featured on various print, online, and radio outlets, including *National Enquirer*, AskMen. com, and *USA Today*. He and Tarantino re-teamed earlier this year with co-author Allie Tarantino for *I Love the Red Sox/I Hate the Yankees*, a baseball humour book on the greatest rivalry in sports history for Triumph Books. In December 2012, his autobiography with Jimmy 'Superfly' Snuka will be released, also by Triumph.

Chattman, who is also a former newspaper editor and reporter, is director of communications for the Music Conservatory of Westchester. His efforts there as well as other endeavours led him to be named one of the 'Rising Stars – Westchester's Forty Under Forty' by The Business Council of Westchester.

Chattman currently resides in Westchester County with his wife Alison and his little Hulkamaniac Noah.

Rich Tarantino is a noted author and wrestling enthusiast. He is the co-author, with John Chattman, of *Sweet 'Stache: 50 Bad Ass Mustaches and the Faces That Sport Them*, a book chronicling the best celebrity mustaches of all time, as well as *I Love the Red Sox/I Hate the Yankees* with both Chattman and co-author Allie Tarantino, a humorous book highlighting the greatest rivalry in the history of sports.

Tarantino currently lives in New York City with his wife Erica and their son Jaxon, and has been a wrestling fan for over 25 years, a passion that began right around the height of the *Tuesday Night Titans* phenomenon.

Barring a close resemblance to NYSWF personality El Bigote, the personal bodyguard of Miele's Mafia during a 'Hair vs. Public Humiliation Match' between Mexi-minis Mascarita Dorada and Pierrothito, the wrestling writer may have had a future in the business if not for his similar build to the long-lost third Mulkey Brother.

That being said, Tarantino's out-of-ring highlights include a memorable spot as one half of the 'United Super Powers', culminating in a tag team duet of the Russian national anthem with WWE Hall of Famer Nikolai Volkoff during the author's final hours as a bachelor.

I want to remember the good, not the bad. I don't dwell on the bad things. It's been an unbelievable situation. I would've never imagined that so many of my friends would not be here – and I mean that in a couple of ways – like because of death, their brains got scrambled or they've had physical disabilities. Their legacy lives on, and hopefully it'll continue to do so. I'm sure if you could ask any of these guys they wouldn't change a thing because

idea so don't blame him. It got over like a lead fart.

The difference between wrestling then and now, and nothing against creating characters and I understand why they do it, but we were just extensions of our own personalities. It had a wonderful lure to the wrestling fan. That is one of the big differences between now and then. But, they can't do it anymore: the name value and TV time they put into them. It's

AFTERWORD

BY TERRY FUNK

the good wasn't just good, it was great in terms of wrestling. I bet even if you asked the guys with serious problems, they wouldn't trade it in for anything.

Here I am going in for my second knee replacement, and hell I wouldn't change it for anything. I've had numerous injuries, and it's made no difference to me. The wonderful things outnumber the bad so much. In terms of gimmicks, I was always looking for some. Terry Funk was a hook in itself, but one time I went to San Antonio with Joe Blanchard and I decided to come out in a mask and then in a couple of weeks I'd reveal myself. I was going to come out as Dr. 'Knows-It-All'. When they'd ask what's my occupation on TV I'd say chiropractor…a bone specialist. It didn't do me any bit of money. When I was in New York, Vince asked me what I wanted to be and I said Chainsaw Charlie. That wasn't Vince's

a worldwide form of entertainment and I understand why they have to control it.

The worst gimmicks ever – the absolute worst probably was Chainsaw Charlie but maybe they were from Jack Pfefer. He was a promoter and he created a ton of guys. He was an absolute idiot who picked his nose all the time. One of the gimmicks he created, and he created hundreds, was Lou Cares? Lou Thesz was champion but he had a card with Lou Cares? on it. He was quite an idiot, but there were a lot of idiots and I loved them all. It was a wonderful, wonderful world of wrestling.